g.u.m. drops
(GRAMMAR, USAGE, & MECHANICS)

90 Reproducible Worksheets Based around Editing
Passages from Classic Literature

by

Melissa L. Schneider

www.inthethinkofthings.com
P.O. Box 391
Williamsfield, IL 61489

ISBN 1-933407-02-6
Printed in the United States
of America
Copyright 2005

Special Thanks to:

Rachel R. Steinbron for the hours she spent helping me by selecting passages as well as editing my "final" copies - your assistance is deeply appreciated.

Dale Solimene and the EDCON Publishing Group for allowing me to use passages from their Classic Worktext Reading Comprehension series. Their help permitted me to get these books out in a much more timely manner than would have been possible otherwise. You may learn more about the EDCON Publishing Group and their products by contacting them at:
30 Montauk Boulevard
Oakdale, New York 11769-1399
(888)553-3266
www.edconpublishing.com

Contents

Complete Sentences 1
Sentence Types 3
Nouns 6
Capitalization 8
Abbreviations 11
Plural Nouns 13
Verbs 16
Verb Tenses 18
Irregular Verbs 21
Contractions 23
Pronouns 26
Possessives 28
Adjectives 31
Adverbs 33
Subject / Verb Agreement 36
Subject / Pronoun Agreement 38
Midterm 45
Prepositions 46
Commas 48, 51, 53, 56
Semi-Colons 58
Quotes 61, 63
Homophones 66
Prefixes and Suffixes 71
Antonyms and Synonyms 76
Expressive Words 81
Sentence Combining 86
Final Examination 90
Teacher's Pages 91

To the Teacher:

The G.U.M. Drops workbooks were designed to be used as daily supplements. Each workbook is exactly 90 pages long and is roughly divided up into 18 weeks. This makes the workbooks ideal to use every day for one semester. However, because the pages continually build upon each other, you can easily adapt the books to fit your schedule by doing more than one page at a time or doing a page every other day. The workbooks were also written directly to the student so they can complete the excercises unassisted. If they do require additional help, there are notes on the answer pages so you can help them work through the concepts.

In the Think of Things reproduction policy is as follows:
We grant to individual purchasers of this book the right to make sufficient copies for use by all students of a single teacher. This permission is limited to a single teacher and does NOT apply to any schools or school systems. Copying this book or its parts in any form for resale is prohibited.

Complete Sentences

A sentence must form a complete thought. To be complete, a sentence must have two parts, a *subject* and a *predicate*.

The **subject** is the part of the sentence that tells us *who* or *what*. The **predicate** is the part of the sentence that tells us *what happened*. Read the following sentence:

The family went to the zoo.

"*The family*" tells us who. It is the subject of the sentence. "*Went to the zoo*" tells us what happened. It is the predicate of the sentence. This sentence has both parts, so it is complete. If one of the pieces was not there, it would not be a complete sentence.

Read the sentences. If they are complete sentences, write a "C" in the blank. If they are not, write an "S" (subject) or a "P" (predicate) to tell which part is there.

Candy is very good.	C	Had to go home.	P
That cute little girl.	S	The gray mouse.	S
He read the book.	C	I drew a picture.	C

Watch out! Sometimes sentences get too long! These are called **run-on sentences**.
Read the run-on sentence below and then make it into shorter sentences.

I woke up on Saturday morning | and remembered I had chores to do | so I got dressed as quickly as I could | because it was warm outside | and I wanted to play | so I had to get my chores finished | so I could go outside and play with my friends | because they were going to go swimming | and I wanted to go with them | because I love swimming.

Read each sentence carefully in this passage from *Dr. Jekyll and Mr. Hyde*. Make sure all of the sentences are complete. If they are not, underline them and write an "S" or a "P" to show which piece is there.

That night, Mr. Utterson could not enjoy his meal, for he was worried about his friend Dr. Jekyll. Mr. Enfield's tale of the strange building made him suspect that the doctor was in deep trouble. <u>After dinner, Mr. Utterson.</u> [S] From a safe, he took a sealed envelope that said "Dr. Jekyll's will." Opening it, Mr. Utterson frowned. <u>Had left everything to his partner, Mr. Hyde.</u> [P] The lawyer remembered how he had refused to give the least help to Jekyll in the making of the will. Now that it was made, though, he took charge of it.

<u>Had been angered by his lack of knowledge about Mr. Hyde.</u> [P] Now it was what he knew about Hyde that bothered him even more. The lawyer thought the will was madness and had warned Jekyll against it. <u>After hearing Mr. Enfield's horrible tale, Mr. Utterson.</u> [P]

Now that you know about complete sentences, you need to know about the different kinds of sentences and how to punctuate them correctly. **All** sentences begin with a capital letter, but they don't all end the same!

TELLING SENTENCES simply tell you something. They end with a period.
She watched the rain pouring down outside.

EXCLAMATORY SENTENCES show strong feeling or emotion. They end with an exclamation point.
I hit a home run!

ASKING SENTENCES ask a question. They end with a question mark.
Have you ever been on an airplane?

Read the sentences below and add the correct punctuation. Some of the sentences may be correctly punctuated more than one way. For example...
   Mark saw a lion.   could be...   Mark saw a lion!   or...   Mark saw a lion?

Add capital letters and ending punctuation to the sentences below.
do you play an instrument
there are a lot of people in this world
the car went speeding by
he yelled, "Run"
is Erica coming to the party
red apples taste better than green apples
suddenly, a light flashed

3

Read each sentence carefully in this passage from *Captains Courageous*. Add capital letters and ending punctuation where needed. Use all three kinds of ending punctuation at least once.

"Do you think I *chose* to come aboard your dirty ship? Of course I'm happy about being saved," continued Harvey, "but the sooner you take me to New York, the better you will get paid."

Harvey pushed his hand down into his pants pocket for some money.

"I've been robbed!" he cried. "I had over a hundred dollars. Give it back!"

The look on the man's face changed. His language became strong.

"If I were *you*, I wouldn't call the boat that helped save you any names. I'm Disko Troop of this fishing schooner, *We're Here*. Disko Troop is no thief and neither is any man aboard. I'm sorry about your money, but a boy your age has no business carrying that much. We cannot go back to New York, and we won't be near land until September."

"It's May," shouted Harvey. "I can't wait until *you're* ready! What am I supposed to do in the meantime?"

"Listen to Dan and help him," answered Disko. "He'll teach you about sea life. I'll pay you ten and a half dollars a month."

Review Time!

Read this passage from *Gulliver's Travels*. Decide whether each sentence is complete or not. If it is not complete, underline it and write an "S" or a "P" above it to tell which part is there. If it is complete, add the correct capitalization and ending punctuation. Make sure and use all three different types of ending punctuation at least once.

The sailing ship was in terrible danger. Strong winds blew it towards the rocks. The sailors and passengers were afraid. What would happen when the ship struck?

One of the passengers, Lemuel Gulliver, was very frightened, but he knew he had to try to save himself.

Crrraaa-aack! Was dashed against the rocks and began to break apart. Some of the men jumped into the water, swimming for their very lives. of them all, only Gulliver reached safety. Climbing out of the water onto the shore of a tiny island, he walked for a while. Then, worn out, he laid down and fell into a deep sleep.

At last Gulliver. He tried to get up, but he found he could not move. What was wrong? He looked down at his body and discovered that he was tied to the ground. it was not rope that held him, but thin cord - a lot of it. Even his hair was fastened to the ground.

Gulliver felt something moving on his leg. he struggled to see and was astonished by what he saw. It was a tiny man less than six inches tall.

Nouns

A noun is a word that names a person, place, or thing.

Common nouns name very general people, places or things. The words below are common nouns.

    lake   dog   friend   state

    movie   chair   jacket   key

Proper nouns name specific people, places, or things. The words below are proper nouns. Titles of books, movies, ships, airplanes, and pets are all proper nouns.

    Lake **E**rie   **R**ex   **D**ave   **K**ansas

    Star **W**ars   **G**randma   **R**ocky **M**ountains   **E.B. W**hite

In the sentences below, underline and capitalize all of the proper nouns.

Who is your favorite football team? I like the green bay packers.

She is going to come and visit. She will drive through new york.

My mom went to the store. denise and kristen went with her.

Can you run for two miles without stopping?

I wish I had a puppy. My friend has a puppy, mischief.

I bought a ticket to go and see the movie the wizard of oz.

My favorite place to go is sand ridge state park.

There weren't very many people at the recital, but nancy came.

I grew up in iowa. I wish that I was from wisconsin.

The apple tree was planted in the middle of our backyard.

Read this passage from *From the Earth to the Moon*. Circle at least ten common nouns. Then underline all of the proper nouns and capitalize them.

The gun club (name of thing) was made up of very nice men. Some of these Gun Club members were officers. Then, one day, the shooting slowed. The war was coming to an end. Then it stopped. Members of the gun club became very bored. The rooms of their club became empty. Sounds of snoring came from dark corners.

"It's disappointing!" tom hunter said one evening. "There's nothing to do! What a weary life!"

"You're right!" spoke colonel bloomsberry.

"No war in sight!" said j.t. maston. He scratched his head. "Only this morning I made a set of plans that will change how wars work!"

"How interesting!" said tom hunter. "Maybe we could build weapons for the wars taking place in europe.

"No," said maston, "that wouldn't work. It seems that americans don't want to take action! For example, didn't america once belong to england?"

"Yes," answered tom.

"Then why shouldn't it be England's turn to belong to america?" said mason.

The club members argued for a long time.

7

Capitalization

There are some other words that need to be capitalized. These words include the days of the week, months of the year, and holidays. Seasons are NOT capitalized.

    November   **T**hursday   **V**eteran's **D**ay   spring

You already know that people's names are capitalized. When people have titles with their names, those are capitalized too.

    Uncle **D**on   **L**ieutenant **H**enry   **P**rofessor **O**bregon

Another word that is capitalized is the word "I." Capitalize it even if it is not at the beginning of a sentence.

    I don't know if **I** want ice cream, but **I** will take some cake.

Read the sentences below and write in capital letters where they belong.

Every thanksgiving, grandma gensch comes to visit.
She has a meeting on wednesday afternoon.
The captain took his orders from general morgan.
Next fall, i will turn 24 years old.
He got his basketball on christmas eve.
Do you think she will work this summer?
I think i will invite pastor mike.
The leaves are prettiest in september.
Is doctor t. billings open on saturdays?
I hope i don't get sick at all in march.

Edit this passage from *Dr. Jekyll and Mr. Hyde*.

"Jekyll," said utterson. "You know I am a man to be trusted. Come clean with this matter, and i will help you."

"Utterson," said the doctor, "this is very good of you, but it isn't as bad as you think. The moment I choose, I can be rid of hyde. Why, i can make him disappear like a magician waving a magic wand."

Utterson thought for a while. "I guess you are right," he said at last, getting to his feet.

"One more thing," continued the doctor. "I really do take great interest in poor hyde. I want you to promise to carry out the will in his favor should something happen to me."

"I can't say that I will ever like Hyde," said the lawyer, sighing, "but, well, i promise."

Nearly a year later, in the month of october, london was startled by the cruel killing of a highly-respected citizen.

Review Time!

Edit this passage from *Twenty Thousand Leagues Under the Sea.*

 When professor aronnax came to new york, people questioned him. He had written a book called "mysteries of the great submarine grounds." The professor was famous for being an expert in this field.

 More and more people asked the professor for his opinion. He gave them this answer. "The ocean deep is not known to us. We do not know of all the creatures that live there. I can only say that there must be a living creature in the sea that is at the bottom of this. It could be as long as sixty feet. With all its power and strength, the creature is doing much harm in our waters."

 The professor's opinion was talked about widely. Because of his knowledge, his opinion was respected by many people.

 The united states made plans to send out a large ship to find the creature. It was called the abraham lincoln. The abraham lincoln had been carefully picked for the voyage. It was a ship of great speed and great strength. The captain of the ship was commander farragut.

Abbreviations

Abbreviations are shorter ways to write words.

We use abbreviations to shorten words. There are abbreviations for many proper nouns, including the days of the week, months of the year, and titles for people. Look closely at the words below and their abbreviations.

Sunday > Sun.   January > Jan.   Mister Favre > Mr. Favre

Abbreviations are usually made by using the first letter and one or more other letters of the original word. Often, the abbreviation is simply the first few letters of that word. Most abbreviations are capitalized and marked with periods. ALL of the abbreviations in this book are capitalized and end with periods.

People's initials are also capitalized and marked with periods. For example:

Thomas A. Edison   P. T. Barnum

In the sentences below, the underlined words can be abbreviated. Write the abbreviations by the words.

Sometimes it snows a lot in February. *Feb.*

Mr. Mister and Misses S. Cox moved across town. *Mrs.*

I have an appointment on Tuesday, June 8th. *Tue Jun*

Are you going to live on Washington Street? *St.*

His father's name was Dean R. Mullins, Senior. *Sr.*

Dr. Doctor Rawlins fixed my broken leg. *Doc*

There should be an extra Friday for every Monday. *Fri Mon.*

Mrs. Miss Penn took a picture of Riverside Avenue. *Ave.*

Edit this passage from *Dr. Jekyll and Mr. Hyde*.

"I must get to the bottom of this!" said Mr Utterson, as he put on his coat and went out into the icy london night. He headed in the direction of cavendish square, where his friend the great dr. Lanyon had his home. Dr Lanyon was also an old friend of Dr. jekyll's. "If anyone knows more about this curious matter, it will be Lanyon," utterson thought.

"I suppose, lanyon," said Mr. Utterson, "you and I must be the two oldest friends that henry Jekyll has."

dr. Lanyon's face took on a curious appearance. "Yes, i suppose we are. What of it? I see little of him now."

"Indeed?" said Utterson. "I thought you worked together."

"We did," answered Lanyon, "but it is more than ten years since Henry jekyll has become too mad for me. He began to go wrong, wrong in the mind." Dr Lanyon shook his head. "Such nonsense in these modern days."

mr Utterson decided to ask the question he had come to put. "Did you ever come across a partner of Jekyll's, a hyde?"

"Hyde?" repeated Dr. lanyon. "No. Never heard of him."

Plural Nouns

Plural nouns name more than one person, place, or thing.

You can make most nouns plural just by adding an "**s**."

    tree > tree<u>s</u>　　　building > building<u>s</u>　　　duck > duck<u>s</u>

If a noun ends with "**ch**," "**sh**," "**s**," "**x**," or "**z**," add "**es**" to make it plural.

    lunch > lunch<u>es</u>　　　sash > sash<u>es</u>　　　box > box<u>es</u>

If a noun ends with a **consonant** and then a "**y**," change the "**y**" to an "**i**" and add "**es**."

    bunny > bunn<u>ies</u>　　　story > stor<u>ies</u>　　　sky > sk<u>ies</u>

If a noun ends with a "**v**" or an "**f**" that makes a "**v**" sound in the plural, add "**es**."

    calf > calves　　　loaf > loaves　　　life > lives

Some plural nouns don't follow any rules at all. Here are some **irregular plural nouns**.

    mouse > <u>mice</u>　　　child > <u>children</u>　　　ox > <u>oxen</u>

Read the sentences below and write the plural nouns in the blanks provided.

There was a white house. There were two white _____.

I used a match to light the fire. I used two _____ to light the fire.

We have one library in town. We have two _____ in town.

A woman was walking by. Two _____ were walking by.

Did you see that blue bus? Did you see those two blue _____ ?

There was a knife on the table. There were two _____ on the table.

Read this passage from *The Pathfinder*. Cross out any misspelled plural nouns and rewrite the correct word above it.

"My good friendes are pleased to help me bring you to your father's fort. Jasper owns a large boat and helps the British move their soldiers from place to place. Big Serpent is a brave and famous chief." Pathfinder pointed to the deers cooking over the fire. "Eat with us. Then we'll start off."

Pathfinder moved to whisper into the ear of Mabel's uncle. "We need your help, sir. The forest is alive with our enemys, the Iroquois. Cast your glance into the deep darkness of the forest and let us know if you see something."

Mabel's uncle replied, "Aye. I'll keep a sea watch. Never you fear! I can see a bit of light miless away on the open ocean. I admit, this forest is different, but it's nothing that I can't manage."

Review Time!

Edit this passage from *David Copperfield*.

One morning Peggotty said, "Come along now, master davy. You're coming to my house for awhile."

"Mama can't live alone," I told her.

"She's staying with a friend," Peggotty explained There were tears in Mama's eyes as she waved good-bye. Soon I forgot about Mama and the awful Mr Murdstone. "Over there is my brother's house," Peggotty said, pointing to a barge by the bay.

"This boat is his *house* " I asked. "It's wonderful!" I even liked the fishy smell. Her brother, mr. Peggotty, was a fisherman. Loved all who shared his funny house. With them lived an orphan girl, little emily, and an orphan boy, Ham. Ham was older than Emily. He was six foots tall, with strong arms used for hard work. Little Emily wore blue beads and had beautiful hair. I could tell that Ham loved Emily.

Verbs

Verbs are words that show action.

In the sentences below, the underlined words are verbs.

    She <u>hit</u> the ball hard.   Outside, the rain <u>fell</u>.

    The turtle <u>crawled</u> away.   Tim <u>read</u> his book.

Some verbs simply complete a thought. These verbs are called **linking verbs**. They link words together to complete sentences.

    He <u>was</u> a good boy.   I <u>am</u> tired.

"*Was*" links "he" to "good boy." "*Am*" links "I" to "tired." The most common linking verbs are IS, AM, ARE, WAS, and WERE. There are also verbs that "help" an action verb, called **helping verbs**. Linking verbs become helping verbs when they are used with action verbs. The main verbs and helping verbs are underlined in this sentence:

    We <u>are</u> <u>cleaning</u> the house, and then she <u>is</u> <u>coming</u> over.

Read the sentences below and circle all of the verbs. Remember to look for action verbs, linking verbs, and helping verbs.

The boy climbed up the ladder.

Coleen was excited.

The horse ran through the stable.

They are bringing dessert.

Miles listened to the crickets.

We will find the perfect present.

Edit this passage from *Gulliver's Travels*. Also circle as many verbs as you can find, including at least two linking verbs, three helping verbs, and three action verbs.

    The man, armed with a bow and arrow, was walking on Gulliver's leg. He was followed by many others just like him.

    Startled, gulliver cried out.

    The band of tiny men jumped off his body in a hurry. To them, Gulliver was a giant and his cry of surprise was a roar. Gulliver struggled against the cords. He was able to free his left arm. At this, shouts of alarm rose around him. Hundreds of tiny bowss were raised. Gulliver was showered with arrows. They felt like needles in the skin of his arm.

    Gulliver lay back, his arm hurting terribly. He would do nothing more to frighten the little folk around him. He waited quietly

Verb Tenses

Verbs tell what happened in the past, what is happening right now, and what will happen in the future.

Verbs show action in three different **tenses**. This verb is in **past tense.**

    She played the trumpet when she was younger.

This tells us that she played sometime in the past. Past tense verbs often end in **-ed**.

These verbs are in **present tense**. Present tense verbs often end with an **-s** or **-ing**.

    She plays the trumpet.   She is playing the trumpet.

These tell us that she plays the trumpet right now.

These verbs are in **future tense**. They have helping verbs with them.

    She will play the trumpet.   She shall play the trumpet.

These tell us that she will play the trumpet sometime in the future.

Write the tense of the underlined verbs in the blanks provided.

He ate his lunch.   _____

The monkey is sleeping.   _____

Arthur will play tomorrow.   _____

The woman shall walk her dog.   _____

The bird sang a song.   _____

Diane is sick.   _____

I looked at my watch.   _____

Those boys will be at the movie.   _____

Read this passage from *The Time Machine*. Circle as many verbs as you can find and write "past," "present," or "future," by them to show the tense.

"I have invented a machine that I think will travel through time," our friend told us. At first, no one said anything. Our friend liked to make jokes, but tonight he looked very serious. It was also true that he was an inventor. Even the chairs we were sitting in were not ordinary chairs, but his own special design.

Then one of the other guests laughed. "Travel through time?" he chuckled. "That is not possible."

"That is what everyone thinks," our friend replied, nodding. "Perhaps that is why no one has ever bothered to try."

There was more laughter.

"If you do not believe me," our friend said, "I guess I will have to show you."

"Here," our friend answered. Looking closely, we saw that his hands did contain a small metal object. He explained that it was just a model of the machine he had talked about, but it would really work.

Review Time!

Edit this passage from *Twenty Thousand Leagues Under the Sea*. Also identify at least two past tense, two present tense, and two future tense verbs.

Three hours before the Abraham Lincoln was to set sail, Professor Aronnax received a letter. it was worded as follows:

Sir:
Will you join the Abraham Lincoln in our search for the great creature The government of the United States will be happy to have you on our voyage. A cabin will be ready for you.

Up until he received the letter, Professor Aronnax longed to go home to france. He wanted to see his home, his country, and his friends. After reading the letter, all professor aronnax could think about was finding the sea creature. Finding it was to become his biggest wish in life.

Irregular Verbs

Irregular verbs do not have an -ed ending in the past tense.

Although many past tense verbs end with **-ed**, there are some verbs that don't. These verbs are called **irregular verbs**. They don't follow any rules, so you will have to learn the ones you don't already know. Here are some common irregular verbs:

am > was	begin > began	come > came
do > did	eat > ate	break > broke
go > went	know > knew	fall > fell
see > saw	speak > spoke	shine > shone
run > ran	think > thought	write > wrote

Fill in the blanks with the past tense of the verbs in parentheses.

A butterfly (fly) _____ by my window yesterday.

My uncle (give) _____ me a big hug.

(Do) _____ you see the newspaper today?

The women (speak) _____ quietly while the baby slept.

Dory (write) _____ her name at the top of the page.

The little girls (sing) _____ very loudly.

The chickens (eat) _____ all of their feed.

I (give) _____ Mitch a high five as he (run) _____ by.

They (are) _____ tired until they (take) _____ their naps.

Edit this passage from *From the Earth to the Moon*. Change any incorrect irregular verbs to the correct words.

The very next day, each member of the club received the following message:

Baltimore, October 3

The president of the Gun Club has the honor of telling his friends that during the meeting on october 5, he will make an announcement that they will be very interested in. He insists that they all be at the meeting.

Impey barbicane, President

October 5th comed. All the members crowded into a hall. It was a big meeting. Models of cannons, rifles, and other war weapons filled the hall. A huge iron desk ised at the far end of the room. Behind it sitted the president of the club, impey Barbicane. The club members knowed he would not have insisted they be there unless it was very important.

Impey Barbicane was a quiet, cold, serious man   He was a true Yankee. He had maked a fortune in the lumber business. He standed out from the other men.

Contractions

A contraction is a shorter way to write two words.

Some words can be joined together with an apostrophe (') to make one shorter word. These shorter words are called **contractions**. The apostrophe goes where the missing letters were.

Many common contractions include the words NOT, IS, AM, ARE, WOULD and WILL. The pronouns I, YOU, WE, THEY, HE, and SHE are also often used in contractions.

| it is | > | it's | they are | > | they're | do not | > | don't |
| I am | > | I'm | he would | > | he'd | she will | > | she'll |

In the sentences below, circle the pairs of words that can be made into contractions. Write the contractions in the blanks provided.

It was not a dangerous dinosaur. _____

I will take off my shoes before I enter. _____

She promised that she would read my favorite book. _____

Do you know if they are happy? _____

Ian did not think it was cold outside. _____

The snow blew harder than I had ever seen it blow. _____

This is not what I had in mind. _____

Do you think it is a good idea? _____

Liz thought he had gone to the store. _____

Edit this passage from *From the Earth to the Moon*. Also circle any pairs of words that can be made into contractions and write the contractions.

"My friends, we have been at peace for too long a period! We must take action! Any war that would bring back the use of weapons would be welcome!" speaked Barbicane.

The members yelled in support.

Barbicane continued, "For now, war is not possible. We must accept this and find another way to use our energy. For a long time I have been thinking of a plan. this plan will make a great noise in the world."

"A great noise?" the colonel asked with great excitement.

"You have all seen the moon, have not you?" barbicane asked. "Well, I will lead you weary men on an adventure. An adventure to the moon "

The crowd cheered! Each member of the club was excited by Barbicane's words.

The voices died down. Barbicane spoke again, this time in a deeper voice. "You all know how firearms have improved these last few years. With this in mind, i started to wonder if it would be possible to build a huge cannon. A cannon large enough to shoot something to the moon. I have looked at it carefully. I think we can succeed! My good friends, let us do it!"

Review Time!

Edit this passage from *Captain's Courageous*. Fix any errors you can find, including capitalization, punctuation, or incorrect past tense verbs. Circle any pairs of words that can be made into contractions and write the contractions.

   Harvey entered Disko's cabin and standed before the captain. "I have not acted quite right, and I am here to say I am sorry," said Harvey, surprised at his own quiet tone.
   Disko standed up and holded out the largest hand harvey had ever seen. "You will make a man yet if you go on this way," said Disko.
   Disko shaked Harvey's hand, cutting off the feeling halfway up Harvey's arm. "Go about your business now," said Disko
   Harvey made his way to the deck to see Dan.
   "Well, I am glad that is settled," said Dan, "but you have got a lot to learn." dan began to show Harvey the parts of the schooner.
   "Guess i have," said Harvey, as he stared out thoughtfully over the shining sea.

Pronouns

Pronouns take the place of nouns.

Instead of using the same noun over and over again, we replace them with **pronouns**. Here is a list of pronouns:

| I | us | me | you | he | him |
| her | she | it | they | them | we |

There are two kinds of pronouns, **objective pronouns** and **subjective pronouns**.

An **objective pronoun** replaces a noun that is an object in the sentence. For example:

    Nate liked the picture.   >   Nate liked it.

    Rain fell on the crowd.   >   Rain fell on them.

A **subjective pronoun** replaces a noun that is the subject of a sentence. For example:

    Nate liked the picture.   >   He liked the picture.

    My family was in the crowd. > We were in the crowd.

The following are **objective pronouns**: me you him her it us them

The following are **subjective pronouns**: I you he she they it

Choose the correct pronouns in the sentences below.

After the meeting, (they / them) drove home. I went with (they / them).

(We / Us) went on vacation. The hotel gave (we / us) reservations.

(Her / She) made some chocolate candy. It took (her / she) all day.

No one can help (I / me) set the table. (I / Me) will do it by myself.

Edit this passage from *The Pathfinder*. Circle the correct pronouns.

The group canoed down the river until (they / them) saw Big Serpent waving on the shore. Pathfinder steered toward (he / him). Big Serpent had seen fresh tracks of the Iroquois

At once, Pathfinder taked charge. "Jasper, (you / they) go up river and set a campfire. (They / Them) will think we've made camp there. Big Serpent, you go back into the woods. Watch what happens. I'll take mabel and the others downstream to that little beach. Do you know where (me / I) mean "

The young man and Indian nodded. (They / Them) took off in different directions.

Pathfinder and Arrowhead guided the two canoes to the beach. They cut tree branches and bushes to make a cover for everyone to crouch under. Soon, Jasper and Big serpent joined (they / them) under the leafy tent. Just then, three Iroquois walked onto the beach.

As the three Iroquois comed near to where they hid, Pathfinder and Jasper heard them speak. They were planning to capture Mabel. (Her / She) would become an Indian's wife!

Possessives

Possessives show that something belongs to someone.

Most possessive nouns are formed by adding an **'s**.

>That fish belongs to my neighbor. It is my neighbor's fish.

>The rope belongs to that cowboy. It is the cowboy's rope.

If the noun is **plural and ends with an "s,"** just add an apostrophe (').

>That rope belongs to those cowboys. It is the cowboys' rope.

Proper nouns can also show ownership. They are capitalized and follow the rules.

>The car belongs to Jess. It is Jess's car.

There are also **possessive pronouns**, which replace possessive nouns.

>It is the dog's ball. It is his ball.

>That is the girls' paper. That is their paper.

Write a possessive noun or pronoun in the blanks provided.

That computer belongs to my dad. It is _____ computer.

This pizza belongs to that family. It is _____ pizza.

That chair belongs to me. It is _____ chair.

This candy belongs to Mindy. It is _____ candy.

That plant was given to Alice. It is _____ plant.

This bunk bed belongs to my brothers. It is _____ bed.

The shelf belongs to Wes. It is _____ shelf.

Edit this passage from *Dr. Jekyll and Mr. Hyde*. Circle any possessive nouns or pronouns you can find.

"Scotland Yard," said the officer. "(We / Us) wish to see Mr Hyde's rooms."

One could see it was a thrill for the woman to hear this. "Ah," she muttered, "he is in trouble."

The men found hyde's place torn apart. Clothes were thrown about, and coins were scattered on the floor Some papers had been burned. From the ashes, the officer pulled part of a check book. The other half of the cane was found behind the door.

The officer was thrilled. "Hyde is in our hands now!" he shouted. "He has money in the bank. All we must do is wait for (he / him) to cash a check!"

This was not to happen. Utterson remembered jekyll's words. "Perhaps," thinked the lawyer, "the magician had waved his magic wand."

Review Time!

Edit this passage from *The Time Machine*. Choose the correct pronouns and circle any possessive nouns or pronouns you can find.

    He let us look at the model as long as (we / us) wished. Then he told us to watch carefully. Setting the tiny machine on the table, he asked one of our friends to push the bar he had shown us before. The Time Traveller taked the guest's hand. The inventor did not have time to coax and tug at the surprised man.

    At last the guest touched his finger to the shiny bar. For one second, the machine trembled as if (they / it) were about to do a somersault. Then, right before our eyes, right beneath his shaking hand, the Time Machine disappeared

.

    "On this machine," our friend said quietly, "I will explore time. I was never more serious in my life."

    There was a long silence. I was not at all sure what i thought.

    The next week we went to our friend's house again for dinner. There we finded a note from (he / him) saying that he had gone out.

Adjectives
Adjectives are words that describe nouns.

Adjectives tell us something about nouns. Adjectives can tell us what size, how many, what color, about texture or shape, and more. The following words are adjectives.

furry   **round**   **yellow**   **fifteen**
sharp   **plastic**   **huge**   **flat**

If you can't decide if a word is an adjective or not, try putting it before a simple noun like "man." Although it may not make much sense - a purple man? - you will be able to tell if it is a describing word or not.

There are other kinds of adjectives. Just remember that all adjectives describe nouns.

Articles -There are three articles, "**A**," "**An**," and "**The**."

Demonstrative -These include words such as "**This**," "**That**," "**These**," and "**Those**."

Comparative and Superlative -These adjectives are use to compare two or more nouns, and they often end in **-er** and **-est**. For example, if you are talking about the different sizes of things, you may use words like "**smaller**," "**bigger**," and **largest**." Watch out for irregular comparative and superlative adjectives!

good > better > best   many > more > most   bad > worse > worst

Circle all of the adjectives in the sentences below.

The little mouse scurried through a tiny hole in the old barn.

That nice, ripe tomato is bigger than an apple!

Those three houses were very neat and clean.

I know this trip was a bad one, but was it the worst trip you've been on?

Carefully read through this passage from *Gulliver's Travels* below. Circle as many of the adjectives as you can find. Remember all of the different kinds of adjectives!

Captain Farragut was a good sea captain. His ship and he were one. The monster responsible for terror on the high seas put Captain Farragut into action. He promised to rid the waters of the great monster.

The officers and crew on the Abraham Lincoln shared the same opinion as the captain. They wanted to meet up with the monster. They would catch up with it and bring it on board. Then they would cut it up. This was the object of the voyage.

Captain Farragut offered two thousand dollars to the first man to spot the monster. Everything needed to catch it was on board.

Captain Farragut had the good sense to have Ned Land, "King of the Harpooners," come along on the trip. Ned was from Canada. He was a large man of great strength. Ned had a no-nonsense manner about him. He did not believe that there was a living creature that was trying to destroy ships at sea.

Adverbs

Adverbs are words that describe verbs, adjectives, or other adverbs.

Adverbs are very similar to adjectives, except they describe words other than nouns.

Many adverbs end with **-ly**. Here are a few examples of the way adverbs can be used:

 The turtle did **not** move **quickly**.   (Adverbs "not" and "quickly" describing verbs)

 The turtle was **extremely** slow.   (Adverb describing adjective, "slow")

 The turtle moved **very slowly**.   (Adverb "very" describing adverb "slowly")

Adverbs can tell when, where, how, how often, and how much or little.

 The boy smiled **first**. (when)   The boy laughed **constantly**. (how often)

 The boy stepped **back**. (where)   The boy sneezed **loudly**. (how)

 The boy **barely** noticed. (how much or little)

There are also **comparative** and **superlative** adverbs. For example:

 Cara swings higher than Todd, but Max swings highest of all.

 I went more than you, but she went most of all.

Circle the adverbs in the sentences below.

The grizzly bear growled loudly at the cold wind.

His sister rarely went to the movies.

The caterpillar inched upwards.

I did not step inside the door.

The flowers will be blooming very shortly.

He rode the bus daily.

Read this passage from *David Copperfield*. Circle all of the adverbs you can find, as well as at least five adjectives.

My two-week visit with Peggotty passed quickly. "I don't want to leave," I cried, with a shiver. I thought of Mr. Murdstone's mean face.

"It is time," Peggotty said, "so don't be a baby."

"I'll miss you," I told Emily. We waved to each other as the carriage headed toward the Rookery.

At home again, a strange servant greeted us. I cried, "Where's Mama?" Something was terribly wrong; I could feel it! My legs began to shake, and I cried, "Has Mama died?"

"Quiet," Peggotty said, adding seriously, "your mother has remarried." Then Mama's arms were around me, and I hugged her very hard.

"Clara," said Mr. Murdstone, "now don't forget. Boys need a strong hand." I felt Mama shiver as she showed me to my new room.

Review Time!

Read this passage from *Gulliver's Travels*. Circle at least three adverbs and at least five adjectives. Underline any possessive nouns or pronouns.

A man wearing robes and a crown came. He stood on a stage the little men had built near Gulliver's head.

"I am Golbasto Gue, mighty king of Lilliput. You have entered my kingdom," he shouted.

"My name is Lemuel Gulliver," said Gulliver. He spoke softly so that he would not hurt the king's ears. "I am a poor traveler from England. My ship has crashed on the rocks, and I fear that all on board her have died. Please bring me food. I am very hungry."

The king called for food.

The people brought barrels of drink and baskets of meat and bread. These they emptied into Gulliver's mouth. He ate and drank all of it and asked for more.

Once again, Gulliver fell into a deep sleep.

Subject / Verb Agreement

The subject and verb of a sentence have to agree.

In present tense, the verb may change depending on the subject. For example:

    Millie **plays** baseball.

In this sentence, there is a singular subject. The verb ends with an "**s**."

    Millie and Cheryl **play** baseball.

In this sentence, there is a plural subject. The verb does NOT end with an "s."

The singular subjects "**I**" and "**You**" do NOT follow this rule. Do NOT add an "s" to the verb when "I" or "You" is the subject.

    I **play** baseball.   You **play** baseball.

Forms of the verb "to be" (IS, AM, ARE, WAS, WERE, DO, DOES, HAS, and HAVE) are confusing in past and present. "**You**" always acts as a plural; "**I**" does sometimes.

  He is late.   I am late.   You are late.   They are late.

  She has a cold.   I have a cold.   You have a cold.   They have colds.

Choose the correct verb in the sentences below.

Denise (hold / holds) the record for the long jump.

They (am / are) going hiking tomorrow.

Sam and Charlie (play / plays) chess a lot.

I (run / runs) a mile every day.

Will you (mop / mops) the floors after the restaurant closes?

The cats (purr / purrs) whenever you pet them.

Edit this passage from *Captains Courageous*. Circle the correct verbs to agree with the subjects as you go.

   The sea was very rough, and he (Harvey) wondered why he was not ill. He asked manuel how much longer the weather would last.
   "Maybe two days, maybe more," said Manuel, winking at Harvey
   Harvey smiled weakly. "A week ago i would have been very sick," he said.
   "Well, you are a fisherman now," said Manuel.
   Fishermen (love / loves) the kind of long talks during which they can (tell / tells) stories and sing sea songs. The talk soon (turn / turns) to shouting, and no one (prove / proves) anything in the end. It was just this kind of talk that Harvey heard on the *We're Here*. Dan beginned with the first two lines of a cheerful rhyme, and one by one, each man joined in, adding to the story. Harvey sitted back and gave his full attention to the mans. Soon their songs made him forget everything but the sea.

Subject / Pronoun Agreement

Pronouns must agree with the nouns they replace.

When you replace a nouns with a pronoun, you must make sure that it agrees with the noun it is replacing.

    <u>The girl</u> was reading *a book*. <u>She</u> was enjoying *it*.

In this sentence, "**The girl**" is replaced by the pronoun "**she**." "**A book**" is replaced by the pronoun "**it**." Both of these are correct.

In the following sentence, the pronouns are NOT correct. They do NOT agree with the nouns they are replacing.

    <u>The ducks</u> waddled past *the boy*. <u>It</u> waddled right by *her*.

The correct pronoun for "**The ducks**" is "**they**," because there is more than one. The correct pronoun for "**The boy**" is "**him**," not "her."

Choose the correct pronouns in the sentence below.

Do you like **spinach**? (She / It) is good for you.

I watched the little **boys** play. I had to watch (them / him) closely.

The **butterfly** flew across the meadow. (It / They) was beautiful.

The **woman** walked to the **store**. (Him / She) went inside (them / it).

You should put your **coat** on. (It / He) will keep you warm and cozy.

The **man** took out his **keys**. (He / She) needed (it / them).

Those **kids** caught that **fish**. (They / He) caught (he / it) in the stream.

Edit this passage from *From the Earth to the Moon*. Choose the correct pronouns as you go.

The same night barbicane announced his plan, the telegraph wires sent messages to distant places around the country   The whole country swelled with pride.

The next day, over 1,500 newspapers carried news of the plan. Persons wondered if the moon was a complete planet; if (they / it) was changing at all. Was it like the earth had been before people lived there? What did the side that couldnt be seen from the earth look like? All that had been planned so far was to send something to the moon. Every newspaper saw this as the start of many experiments. they hoped someday the earth would unlock the last secrets of the moon's world.

Next, preparation began for the big event. First, Barbicane called members of the Gun Club together. (She / They) agreed to talk with some astronomers. together, (they / he) worked out the finishing touches of the plan.

Review Time!

Edit this passage from *Twenty Thousand Leagues Under the Sea*. Circle the correct pronoun or verb in each pair.

The professor (were / was) excited at finding the monster and happy to be saved at the same time. His strength was just about to run out when Conseil came along and saved him.

Conseil helped professor aronnax swim to the "floating island." Another hand reached out to help (it / them). To their surprise, it was Ned Land. Had he also been thrown overboard

(Them / They) soon discovered that the island was made of steel. The monster they had been searching for was made of hard-plate steel! The professor was excited and curious at the same time. (He / They) was happy they had continued on in their search for the monster.

"i have been on this monster for three hours. I have seen no sign of life," said ned. "Let us explore together," he added. The three men beginned to explore the surface of the steel monster.

Edit this passage from *Dr. Jekyll and Mr. Hyde*.

It was late in the afternoon when Mr Utterson found his way to Jekylls door. He was let in by Poole, the butler, and led across a yard to the laboratory. It was the first time mr. Utterson had been in that part of the doctor's house, so he looked at everything with great interest

A fire burned in the fireplace. Close to the warmth sitted Dr. Jekyll, looking deathly sick. (They / He) did not rise to greet his visitor, but he held out a cold hand and welcomed him in a changed voice.

"(Has / Have) you heard about the killing?" asked Mr. Utterson.

The doctor shivered. "(They / It) were shouting the news in the street," he said.

"One word," said the lawyer. "Carew was my friend, but so are you, and i want you to know what I am doing. Are you responsible for hiding this fellow "

The doctor raised his handes as if to cover his face.

"Utterson, I promise you," cried Jekyll. "I (gives / give) you my word that I am done with him in this world. He is safe and will never more be heard of."

Edit this passage from *The Pathfinder*.

   Knowing that the Indians could strike at any moment, Jasper keeped thinking about mabel's safety. He jumped at every noise from the forest. They paddled quietly, as the tiniest sound could warn the Iroquois of their whereabouts.

   Mabels heart beat quicker, but (they / she) was not afraid. Her fine blue eyes shone with excitement. She felt ready for whatever would come.

   "Mabel!" whispered Jasper, "have no fear for I... we will protect you."

   "I am a soldier's daughter! I would be ashamed to say i was afraid."

   "Yes, I (know / knows), but also know we will do everything to keep you from harm."

   "I believe you. Jasper, dont worry about my fears. I would never stand in the way of your duty."

   "Ah, the child is worthy of being a sergeant's daughter," whispered pathfinder. "Pretty one, your father and I fighted together many times."

Edit this passage from *The Time Machine*.

As a joke, i said maybe our friend had climbed on his machine, fastened the strap, and gone for a trip through time. One of the guests (was / were) new this week, so we had to explain about the Time Machine. Just as we were telling how the model had seemed about to make a somersault, there was a sound at the door.

In came our friend with his clothess all dirty and torn. He had cuts on his face and walked with a limp. On his feet (he / him) wore only a pair of torn and bloody socks. At first he didnt seem able to speak. He had to tug at my sleeve and point to a glass of water to show that he wanted some. Then he seemed to feel a little better and even smiled.

"What's wrong?" we all asked. "Where (have / has) you been "

He said he was very hungry and would explain everything after he'd eaten.

"Have you been time travelling?" i cried. "Please (tell / tells) us."

"Yes," he answered, and began to eat.

Edit this passage from *David Copperfield*.

Then came a whisper at the door. "Peggotty?" i asked.

"Davy," she said, "be as quiet as a mouse, or the cat will hear!" I knew she meant Mr Murdstone.

"How's Mama?" I asked.

Peggotty cried softly. "You'll see her tomorrow... before you go away."

I stood frozen for a moment. "*Away?*" I asked, my heart beating wildly.

"Yes," peggotty replied, "to a london school."

Her words hit me like a hammer. (Me / I) would be leaving the Rookery. My tears began to fall.

Afraid about what lay ahead, I left for school in the morning. I held tight the cake, money, and the note from mama. Our servant Peggotty had given it to me   At nine years old, I worried about meeting the head professor and the other boys. I was right to have worried. The professor telled everyone I was to blame for hurting Mr. Murdstone.

Midterm

Edit this passage from *From the Earth to the Moon*.

   some people believed that the moon (was / were) once a comet. A few people believed the moon had passed too closely to the earth and had been catched by our gravity. Others believed the moon was coming closer every time it went around the earth. (Them / They) thought (he / it) would one day fall against the earth. Finally, people read enough to know that they were wrong

   Impey barbicane chose a committee from the members to help him carry out his plan. These members (was / were) as follows: Barbicane himself, General Morgan, major Elphiston, and J T Maston. On october 8 they met at Barbicanes house. He spoke first.

   "Gentlemen, we must clear up an important problem. (We / They) must first think about what kind of rocket our cannon will send to the moon "

Prepositions

Prepositions are words that add meaning to sentences by showing location or direction.

In sentences, prepositions help to tell about the position of subjects or objects. There are a lot of different prepositions. Listed below are some common prepositions.

| about | across | at | before | by | for |
| from | through | in | with | of | on |

Prepositions begin **prepositional phrases**. The prepositional phrase includes all of the words from the preposition up to a noun or pronoun, which mark the end of prepositional phrases. In the sentences below, the prepositions are in bold and the prepositional phrase is in italics. Notice that you can have more than one prepositional phrase in a sentence.

The worm ate ***through** the apple*.

The letter is ***from** my mother*. It came ***before** lunch*.

She walked ***around** the desk* and ***into** the main office*.

Circle the prepositions and underline the prepositional phrases.

I laughed at the clown.

My father was standing by the door.

The trash can is inside the cabinet under the sink.

The kittens stayed in the barn during the storm.

The boy mowed carefully around the rose bushes.

She looked across the street.

Read this passage from *The Pathfinder*. Find and underline at least seven prepositional phrases, circling the prepositions.

Finally, Jasper returned with Big Serpent riding in the canoe. Big Serpent told them he'd won the battle with the Indian in the river. Then, he crept back to the Iroquois' camp and discovered that Arrowhead was the Iroquois' friend. Arrowhead was telling the Iroquois all of Pathfinder's plans.

Pathfinder shook his head. "That's why he left me! There is no time to lose. We must get Mabel to the fort. The fastest way is down the Oswego Falls. The Iroquois would never think we'd chance it."

He looked at Mabel and said gently, "Jasper is an expert in these waters, and it will be best if you went in his canoe. Big Serpent will come with me."

Mabel's cheeks grew warm as she moved to handsome Jasper's canoe. The canoe swept along in the dark, and the sound of the falls grew louder and louder.

Jasper spoke into her ear over the noise. "We are here at the falls. I beg you to trust me. We are not old friends, but I feel I have known you for years."

"I feel the same, Jasper, and I do trust you."

Commas

A comma marks a slight pause in a sentence.

Commas are used in many different ways. Here are a few of the ways they are used:

Use commas in large numbers with more than three digits.

946   **1,280**   **547,239**   **32,464**

Use commas to separate the month and day from the year when you write the date.

November 4, 1981   **January 3, 2005**   **May 17, 1611**

Use commas to separate a city and state or country.

Bloomfield, New Jersey   **London, England**

In a letter, use a comma after the greeting and closing. Also, notice that the first word in the greeting and closing of a friendly letter and any names are capitalized.

Dear Grandma,   **Your friend,**   **Sincerely yours,**
                      Renee   **Judy**

Edit this letter by adding capital letters and commas.

dear janine   july 9 1992

  i am sorry that i couldn't come over and play today. i was in denver colorado. is it okay if i come august 2 1995? that is in only 1119 days. please call and let me know if this will work for you.   love

                                                              ray

Edit this letter. It is a made-up letter that Professor Aronnax from *Twenty Thousand Leagues Under the Sea* could have sent to a relative back home.

october 21 1867

dear aunt ruth

Hello! How are you doing? I am doing well. So far our adventure has been dull. We have been at sea for three long months - that's over 2000 hours - with no sighting of the monster. I still am not at all certain what we should be looking for. The captain says we will turn around soon if we do not see anything.

I miss everyone back home in paris france. It is not the same in the united states, although I did very much enjoy new york city new york. It is a very nice city. I will be home sometime in the next year. I will see you then!

sincerely

professor aronnax

Review Time!

Edit this passage from *From the Earth to the Moon*. Also underline at least three prepositional phrases, circling the prepositions.

 There were many questions. The Gun Club mailed a letter to the famous observatory at cambridge massachusetts. The astronomers and scientists there were known around the world. They also had a very powerful telescope. Two days later, the Gun Club received their answer.

                cambridge massachusetts
Mr. Impey Barbicane   october 7
President of the Gun Club
baltimore maryland

 dear Mr. Barbicane
 After receiving your letter, our staff met right away. We answered your questions the best we could.
 The members of the Gun Club must start preparation right away for the launch. If you miss the date, you will not find the moon in the same spot for eighteen more years!
 We at the observatory are ready to help if you have any more questions. We wish you well. You are all the pride of america!
         sincerely
         J M Belfast

Commas

A comma marks a slight pause in a sentence.

Now that we have covered how commas are used in letters, we are going to look at a few other ways they are used.

Commas are used to separate things in a series. This may be a series of nouns, verbs, or even phrases.

    I folded the sheets, towels, and washcloths.

    She rode her bike, played by the pond, and flew her kite.

Commas mark pauses after introductory phrases before the main part of a sentence.

    After the sun went down, we watched the fireworks.

    While my brother did the dishes, I swept the floor.

Commas are used to separate two adjectives. However, you do not need a comma if one of the adjectives is a color or a number.

    The boy wanted a soft, friendly puppy.

    She likes to play with the plastic <u>yellow</u> duck.

Add commas where they belong in the sentences below.

The baby smiled laughed and rolled over.

Were you scared by that loud shrill whistle?

When the girls woke up they made breakfast.

Polly asked for two long ribbons.

Edit this passage from *Twenty Thousand Leagues Under the Sea* by adding commas where they belong.

The professor, Conseil, and Ned walked about hoping to find some signs of life on the floating island. Some time had gone by when they felt a sudden motion. The monster began to move slowly through the icy waters.

It was a long night for the three of them. They held on tightly to the monster for fear of being thrown into the sea. All they could do was hold on tight and wait. The motion did not stop. Their only hope was that the monster would not go beneath the surface of the water. It was a very long, cold night for them.

Morning came. All of a sudden, the motion of the steel monster came to a stop. Some kind of iron plate, like a door, seemed to open up right where they were standing. Eight men of great strength dragged them down into the monster.

Ned, Conseil, and the professor spent much time sleeping. After they woke, they spent a good deal of time talking. Ned became angry.

Professor Aronnax, being a patient man, kept Ned from going into a rage. While the professor was upset, he knew it would be dangerous to do something foolish.

52

Commas

A comma marks a slight pause in a sentence.

Commas are used to mark a pause after an introductory word or a light exclamation at the beginning of a sentence.

    Well, I need to get to bed.   Yes, she is starting school tomorrow.

    Wow, that car is really fast!   Great, I'll see you there!

Commas are used to set off interruptions in a sentence.

    As the day continued, however, I found that I was wrong.

    We are, I think, going to leave in the morning.

Commas are used to mark a pause when someone is spoken to directly. It doesn't matter if they are addressed at the beginning, end, or middle of a sentence.

    Mrs. Clay, can you please pick up some milk?

    The goat has gotten out of the pen again, Harold.

    Have you knit a scarf lately, Adam, or has it been a while?

    I need you, dear girl, to help me.

Add commas to the sentences below.

There are I believe more cookies in the pantry.

Do you want to go skating Marsha or skiing?

Oh that would be nice.

Cara this shirt is for you.

Hey you can't go in there!

Edit this passage from *Dr. Jekyll and Mr. Hyde* by adding commas where they belong.

"I cannot tell you how I know this, but I am sure he will never return," said Jekyll. "There is one thing I would like to ask you, Utterson. I have received a letter from Hyde, and I don't know if I should show it to the police. I should like to leave it in your hands and have you decide."

The letter was signed by Edward Hyde. It said that he was grateful for all of Dr. Jekyll's help, but it would no longer be necessary for the doctor to worry about him. He had a way to escape and would bother no one again.

"Well, you have had a fine escape," continued Utterson. "I'm sure Hyde wanted to kill you and collect the money."

"Oh, more than that," moaned Jekyll, "I have learned something which I shall never forget."

On his way out, Utterson stopped to exchange a word with Poole.

"By the way, Poole," he said. "A letter was delivered by hand today. Who brought it?"

Poole was sure that nothing had come except by mail.

Review Time!

Edit this passage from *Gulliver's Travels* by adding commas where they belong.

In Blefuscu, Gulliver was not so comfortable. There was no chair, bed, or table. He had no cooks to supply his food. Life in Blefuscu would be harder than it had been in Lilliput.

One day, Gulliver was walking along the shore. He saw something large and dark in the water. The rising tide brought it nearer. He saw that it was an empty boat. Not just an empty boat, but a boat his size!

Diving into the water, he swam to the boat and fastened the rope to it. He began to swim for land. It was slow, but the boat was moving toward land. Some Blefuscudian ships joined him, fastening lines to the boat too. Slowly, they approached the beach. At last, the boat was on dry land!

It took a month, but at last the boat was ready. Gulliver was on his way home!

Back home, Gulliver showed off his tiny animals, charging people to see them, and he made a great deal of money. He was not happy, for he longed for excitement. He sold his sheep and cattle. He left the money for his wife and children and, once again, he set out on a ship on a search for adventure.

Commas

A comma marks a slight pause in a sentence.

Commas are used to set off an **appositive**, a word or phrase that renames the noun or pronoun right before it.

    My mother, a nurse, works at the hospital.

    Your little sister, Leah, has a basketball game on Tuesday.

Commas are also used to mark a pause between two **independent phrases** connected by a conjunction - AND, BUT, OR, FOR, NOR, SO or YET. An independent phrase means that it is a complete sentence. Read the following sentence.

    The little boy climbed up the tree, <u>but</u> he couldn't get back down.

This sentence is made from two independent clauses. *"The little boy climbed the tree"* and *"he couldn't get back down"* are both complete sentences.

    The little boy climbed up the tree <u>but</u> couldn't get back down.

Because the second part of the sentence *"couldn't get back down"* has no subject, it is not an independent clause, and no comma is needed.

Add commas where they belong in the sentences below.

She wanted to go to the store and to the bank.

You can have your supper now or you can have it later.

My father that man by the door is always early.

It does not seem very late yet the sun has been down for hours.

Geeves the butler answered the door but there was no one there.

Edit this passage from *David Copperfield* by adding commas where they belong.

Summer passed and when fall came I was allowed a visit to the Rookery. I noticed that Mama seemed ill and she spoke slowly, having to pause often. Her husband Mr. Murdstone made my holiday a bad one, ordering me to stay away from Peggotty.

"So this is Davy!" I heard someone say. I looked up to see a jolly man coming toward me. "I'm Mr. Micawber," he said, as he reached to shake my hand, "and you're going to live with me and my family."

I soon came to learn that the Micawbers could not pay their bills even though Mr. Murdstone sent them money for taking me in. As the weeks passed I offered to share my work money with them.

"We couldn't take your money Davy," Mrs. Micawber said. "You need that money for your food and clothes but you can help."

I helped them get money in that way but it didn't take care of their problems.

Semi-Colons

A semi-colon marks a longer pause in a sentence.

Semi-colons are similar to commas, but when there is a semi-colon it means there is a longer pause than when there is a comma.

One of the rules for <u>commas</u> is to use one when two independent clauses are joined by AND, BUT, OR, FOR, NOR, YET, or SO. If there are two independent clauses that are joined WITHOUT one of these words, then you use a semi-colon and there is a longer pause. For example:

>We have a four-wheeler**,** **but** I'm not allowed to drive it.
>We have a four-wheeler**;** I'm not allowed to drive it.

Another use for the semi-colon is in a series where one or more of the items in the series uses commas already. For example:

>I need to make my bed**;** clean the kitchen**,** bathroom**,** and living room**;** and vacuum the stairs.

Add semi-colons where they belong in the sentences below.

There is a robin in the tree it looks lonely.

Max wants to watch a movie and then go to bed.

The man opened his umbrella it was raining outside.

Kim said she would watch her sister her mother is sick.

The queen ordered the seamstress to make her a dress the baker to bake some pies, cookies, and bread and the maid to polish her crown.

Edit this passage from *Dr. Jekyll and Mr. Hyde* by inserting commas and a semi-colon where they belong.

That night the fog rolled over the streets and wrapped the city in silence. Mr. Utterson and Mr. Guest sat in the lawyer's study enjoying some wine.

Utterson handed Guest the letter. Guest's eyes grew bright as he studied it with great interest.

"No sir," he said. "He's not mad but it is a strange hand."

Just then a servant entered with a note from Dr. Jekyll. "Ah," said Utterson, "Jekyll is inviting me to dinner."

Mr. Guest was familiar with Dr. Jekyll's handwriting after his many years of service to Mr. Utterson. "Could I see the note?" asked Guest.

He put the papers next to each other and looked at them closely. "The two hands are equal in many points they are only differently sloped," he decided.

Guest and Utterson exchanged silent glances. "I would not speak of this note you know," said the master.

"No sir," said the clerk in an equally serious voice.

That night Mr. Utterson locked the note in his safe.

Review Time!

Edit this passage from *The Time Machine.*

At last our friend pushed his plate away and looked around at us. Now he was ready to tell the whole story.

That very morning he said he put the final touches on the Time Machine.

He took a deep breath and a strong grip on the bar and so began his journey into time.

As he watched the world flash white with snow and green with grass he knew he must be travelling almost a year a second. Still he travelled on and on. At last he decided he was ready to stop. Taking hold of the bar which turned off the machine he went head over heels. It was lucky our friend the Time Traveller was tough for he was quite shaken by the fall. He found himself on a soft green lawn with the Time Machine lying on its side near him. A huge white statue stood close by. It looked like an enormous ugly bird with a cruel smile.

Then he heard someone coming. He wondered if it was a party of scouts sent to find out what or who he was. He feared they might try to capture or harm him. As soon as he saw them his fears were at an end. They were lovely little people they were no bigger than children.

Quotes

A quote is the exact words of a speaker.

If someone is speaking, everything they say is a quote. It is only a quote if it is the speaker's exact words. For example:

"I would like to play soccer," Kyle said. "It looks like fun."

This is a quote. Kyle is speaking.

Kyle said that he would like to play soccer because it looks fun.

This is NOT a quote. Someone else is telling us what Kyle said.

Read the following quote.

Kyle said, "I would like to play soccer. It looks like fun."

Notice that quotation marks go on either end of the quote. However, **Kyle said** is not inside the quotation marks, because it is not part of what Kyle said. Also notice that the quotation marks go on the outside of any punctuation.

Read the sentences below. If they are quotes, add quotation marks.

Stay off of my lawn, the neighbor said. I just planted some grass.

Gary replied, Yes, I will fix the door.

The girl said that she was nine.

How old are you? I asked.

My grandpa will tell you that he was a fireman.

Stacy said, It is almost 5 o'clock. We will have to wait.

Edit this passage from *Captains Courageous*.

What's a Jonah? asked Harvey, sensing that it was something important.

A Jonah is anything that brings bad luck. Sometimes it's a man a boy or a bucket, said Tom. There are all kinds of Jonahs, and don't you ever wonder if any of them are true, he told Harvey.

Well in my opinion Harvey is no Jonah, Dan said. The day after he came aboard, we had the best catch of the day.

The cook threw back his head and interrupted Dan with a strange laugh.

One day Harvey will be your master Danny, said the cook.

Master, he said, pointing to Harvey.

Man, said the cook, pointing to Dan.

I'm grateful for the news, said Dan with a laugh. When?

In a few years, answered the cook. It cannot be avoided. Then he turned to finish peeling potatoes and wouldn't say another word.

Dan said that many things would have to happen before that would take place.

Quotes

Here are some rules for punctuating quotes.

The first word of a quote is always capitalized. If the quote is split in the middle of a sentence, as in the second example below, only capitalize the first word of the quote.

    She said, "**S**ummer seems to go by so quickly."

    "**S**ummer is nearly over," she said, "and I will miss it."

    "**T**here isn't much summer left," she said. "**S**oon it will be fall."

Unless there is a question mark or an exclamation point, there is always a comma separating the quote from the speaker. It can come before or after the speaker's name. These commas and ending punctuation always go inside the quotation marks.

    "I am going to make a snowman**,**" the boy said.

    Theresa replied**,** "No, I don't want an apple**.**"

    "Are you leaving**?**" she asked. "It is still early**.**"

    "Watch out**!**" I yelled. "That car isn't going to stop**!**"

Punctuate the sentences below.

Whitney said that she liked balloons.

I cried   wait for me

There aren't   she said   any more cookies in the jar.

I have a big test tomorrow.

Can you come over tomorrow   Sharon asked

Wow   he exclaimed. That was an awesome circus

He looked out the window and said   that is the biggest bird I've ever seen

Edit this passage from *From the Earth to the Moon*. You will need to add capital letters, commas, ending punctuation, and quotes where they belong.

Then, spoke Barbicane, let's take the speed of 2400 feet each second as our starting point. We'll need to increase it times 15. First, let's talk about the design of the rocket itself.

What about it? asked Major Elphiston.

Maston answered it must be very large; large enough for whoever lives on the moon to notice.

Yes, said Barbicane, and also for another important reason.

What do you mean asked the major.

I mean, it is not enough to send off a rocket and then forget about it. We must be able to watch it until it reaches the moon.

What! yelled the general and the major. Then you must be planning on making the rocket huge!

No spoke Barbicane, we'll place a telescope on a high mountain and bring magnification to 48000. That will bring the moon to within five miles. We will be able to see objects only 9 feet wide.

Wonderful cried J.T. Maston.

Review Time!

Edit this passage from *David Copperfield*.

Yes Davy Mr. Micawber said over dinner, we're leaving. We will move to Plymouth and we'll start all over.

"Yes," I thought, "I will start over too. I will run away to my Aunt Betsey's. I know she wished for a boy when I was born... but she is family."

On the sixth day, I arrived at Aunt Betsey's. At first, she was afraid of my dirty sunburned face and hands.

No boys allowed here she cried.

Aunt Betsey, it's me... Clara's child. I'm David Copperfield I said.

After a long pause she waved her hand for me to come closer. It was then that I knew I had to make Aunt Betsey like me.

I wrote to Mr. Murdstone Aunt Betsey said one morning.   She held up a paper, saying, Here is his reply and he's coming for a visit.

Oh no, I said softly.

Speak up, Aunt Betsey cried, smart people don't grumble

Homophones

Homophones are words that sound the same but have different meanings.

There are a lot of homophones, but you are probably already familiar with many of them. Here is a list of common homophones:

red	**>**	**read**	**one**	**>**	**won**	**sum**	**>**	**some**
for	**>**	**four**	**eye**	**>**	**I**	**buy**	**>**	**by**
to	**>**	**too**	**>**	**two**	**there**	**>**	**they're**	**>**	**their**

Circle the correct words in the sentences below.

Cindy wanted (to / too / two) ride her new (read / red) bike to the park, but her mother said (know / no).

My brother went to the movies last (knight / night). I went (to / too / two).

(Eye / I) like to (right / write) stories (for / four) my sisters.

Stan was sitting (by / bye) the tree. (Its / It's) leaves were falling all around (him / hymn).

She (new / knew) she was going to like the (new / knew) girl.

If you ever (sea / see) a dragon, the best thing to (do / dew) is simply to walk right up to it and say, "(It's / Its) nice to (meat / meet) you!"

Edit this passage from *The Pathfinder*.

    Pathfinder saw crouched forms sneaking up (to / too / two) them. He picked mabel up under his arm and retreated to the shelter. He locked the door quickly and checked to make sure the rooms were empty. There was no one June had left.

    Outside, the sergeant called that he had been wounded. Pathfinder and Mabel hurried and pulled (hymn / him) inside.

    The sergeant whispered, "Pathfinder I have (no / know) doubt that you will make Mabel a kind husband. Bless you my daughter for doing as i wish." The sergeant laid back, and Mabel bowed her head in prayer.

Edit this passage from *Twenty Thousand Leagues Under the Sea*.

Finally, the door opened. A steward came in carrying a tray of food. Ned could not help himself   He flew into a rage and knocked the man to the floor.

The men struggled until a voice speaked the following words in perfect English: "Calm down Mr. Land and thank you, Professor Aronnax, for your help. Now if you will please listen to me."

The man who spoke to the prisoners was the captain of the ship. When he heard the man speak Ned was startled. He rose suddenly.

The captain stood with arms folded. He spoke calmly to Ned, Conseil, and the professor. "I owe you three gentlemen an explanation. I was a long time coming to visit you. That was because (I / me) needed to decide what to do with you. You all have caused me much trouble."

The captain spoke, It is by an accident which happened on the waters that you (has / have) found my ship. I have the right to treat you as prisoners. I do not owe you your right to freedom.

Edit this passage from *Gulliver's Travels*.

   Gullivers ship sailed along for many weeks. The sea was calm, and the weather was warm. Then a great storm came up and the wind blew the ship off course. For days, the ship was tossed by huge waves until at last the sailors spotted land.

   They needed fresh water so a small group was sent to the land in a small boat to look for some. Gulliver, wishing to explore, went along.

   He walked along the rocky beach for some time, and when he came back, he saw that the sailors were leaving without him, rowing the boat with all (his / their) might toward their ship. Then he saw what had happened to horrify them so. A giant was chasing them

   Gulliver was left behind. He hurried away from the beach. He must find a place to hide! Soon he found himself in a field of corn. It was huge. Each plant (was / were) as tall as a tree. Suddenly, he saw more giants!

   He trembled in fear as they approached. Why had he left the safety of england? Why had he ever left his cozy home   Now he knew how the Lilliputians had felt about him.

Edit this passage from *Dr. Jekyll and Mr. Hyde*.

Thousands of pounds (was / were) offered in reward for Mr Hyde. Hyde had disappeared as if he had never lived. Terrible storys were told about him. He had stolen had often been in fights and had been cruel to everyone.

A new life began for Dr. Jekyll. He taked great delight in being with his friends. He gave to the poor and was often seen at church. His face seemed to open and brighten and there was a gleam in his eyes. For more than (to / too / two) months, the doctor was at peace.

Mr. utterson saw Dr. Jekyll almost every day. Then, one afternoon in january, the door was shut against him. Poole told the lawyer that the doctor was not receiving guests.

Prefixes & Suffixes

A prefix is a group of letters that can be added to the beginning of words.

A suffix is a group of letters that can be added to the end of words.

Prefixes and suffixes are used in many words. You should recognize most of them. Read through the examples below and try to come up with some other words that also use those prefixes and suffixes.

One common prefix is "**un**." It means "not." It is used with a lot of different words. Here are some words that begin with this prefix.

unhappy   >   Paul was unhappy when he was chosen last. (not happy)

unhealthy   >   My mom said that the snack was unhealthy. (not healthy)

You already know some common suffixes, such as "**ed**" (past tense verbs) and "**er**" and "**est**" (comparative adjectives). Another common suffix is "**ful**." It means "full of."

care**ful**   >   Sarah was careful not to spill her water.   (full of care)

thank**ful**   >   The family was very thankful for the meal. (full of thanks)

Read the sentences below and circle any prefixes or suffixes. Try and figure out what the prefixes and suffixes mean.

She had to return the books to the library.

The boy ran swiftly to his tricycle.

Dawn thought the previews were funnier than the real movie.

My coauthor is very capable.

The actress joyfully read her script.

Edit this passage from *From the Earth to the Moon*.

On october 20, an important contract was signed. It was with the cold spring company. The contract said that this company would be in charge of making the cannon. They would make arrangements to hire all the workers. The work was to be done (buy / by) October 15th of the next year. The cannon would be made in Tampa Florida.

On September 30, at 3:47 P.M., a message was delivered to Barbicane. It came by cablegram. He opened the envelope and (read / red) the message. His lips turned pale. This is what was written:

                                                Paris France
                                                September 30

Barbicane
Tampa Florida, U.S.A.

Replace the cannon shell you have, and put in a lighter shell instead. *I* will go to the moon in it. I will come on the ship named *atlantic*.

                                                  Michel Ardan

Edit this passage from *The Time Machine*.

The sun set The gray of the evening grew into darkness, and Weena was afraid. The Time Traveller, trying to calm her fears, talked until he was (hoarse / horse). He was no longer sure of his direction in the dark so the Time Traveller decided to rest there until morning. Weena slept, wrapped in his jacket, while he listened for Morlocks.

As soon as dawn came they started off again. The Time Travellers foot was so sore that he took off his shoes and throwed them away. Then he went on, hoping to find something that he could use to break open the base of the white statue. he wanted his Time Machine back and to return to his own time right away.

Edit this passage from *Captain's Courageous*.

Meanwhile, Harvey Cheyne, Senior, was in his home in San Diego California, trying to take care of his business and his wife. Ever since Harvey had been lost at sea, Mrs Cheyne had become half-mad and needed the care of doctors and nurses. Harvey Cheyne thought of his son often, and his business became less and less important to him.

After three days fifteen and a half hours and 2350 miles, the train arrived at the station. Harvey was waiting for them.

Harvey Cheyne, Senior, looked at his son closely. What he saw pleased him. He remembered what his son had been like - fresh unhappy and just plain difficult. The boy in front of him now looked at him with clear steady eyes. The boy was a pleasant young man who spoke in a voice that said the new Harvey had come to stay.

Harveys parents visited the wharf the next day. Dan went around introducing the Cheynes to the crew. Mrs. Cheyne was especially happy to meet Manuel when she found out he (had / have) saved her son.

74

Edit this passage from *David Copperfield*.

Not only had I lost my job, but my boss wouldnt return aunt Betsey's money - the money she had paid him for my training. I knew both my aunt and my future wife Dora believed that i could become a success. This helped me to rise early the next day to hunt (for / four) a job. Perhaps one of the professors could use the help of someone like (I / me). After all, I once was a schoolboy myself.

I walked to a nearby school and found the head professor's office. "Don't hesitate," I told myself. "Just go in and make your speech."

To my joy, I got the job I worked days and evenings helping to mark papers. Being at the school made me think of Traddles and I decided to pay him a visit.

Hello, old man, Traddles said. "Do you always rise this early in the day?"

I smiled at his sleepy face. "No but from now on that will be my habit, as I've found a new job."

Antonyms & Synonyms

Antonyms are words that have opposite meanings.

Synonyms are words that have the same meaning.

If you are looking for the antonym of a word, you are looking for a word that is exactly the opposite. The antonym of "long" is "short."

> The girl had **long** hair.
> The girl had **short** hair.

If you are looking for a synonym of a word, you are looking for a word that means almost exactly the same thing. A synonym for "jump" is "hop."

> I saw the frog **jump** into the pond.
> I saw the frog **hop** into the pond.

Read the sentences below and write antonyms and synonyms for the underlined words in the blanks provided.

	ANTONYMS	SYNONYMS
The boy thought it was hot outside.	_____	_____
The clown was happy.	_____	_____
It was a very big tree.	_____	_____
The cloud was below the sun.	_____	_____
She ran across the finish line.	_____	_____
Karen smiled.	_____	_____
The math problem was easy.	_____	_____

Edit this passage from *Twenty Thousand Leagues Under the Sea*.

    At the end of captain Nemo's guided tour of the *Nautilus* (name of ship), he pointed to a large map on the wall.

    The captain spoke. "We are three hundred miles from japan. It is twelve noon on November 8 1867. We will now begin our underwater journey around the world."

    Captain Nemo left the professor alone The professor was deep in thought. He was just about to leave the area when all the lights went out. He heard a noise. There were (to / too / two) sliding panels opening. There was one on each side of the ship.

    The professor saw to his surprise two large windows. The water outside (was / were) lit up for miles. A beam of light went out as far as the professors eyes could see.

    "What a view of the ocean floor!" thought the professor. It was like looking out into a giant aquarium.

Edit this passage from *Gulliver's Travels*.

There was a cry from above. He (Gulliver) heard people moving about. A voice called down, "If (their / there / they're) be anybody below, let them speak!"

"It is i, Lemuel Gulliver! Please save me from this terrible prison "

"This is the captain! Be of good spirit. You will soon be saved. We must cut a hole in the top of the box," came the answer

gulliver protested, "No! One of you must put his finger through the ring! If you lift my box out of the water, I can come through the door!"

Someone laughed. "He must think us giants!"

Soon afterward a hole was sawed in the top of the box. Gulliver was taken out.

"You are not Brobdingnagians! You are no taller than I!" said Gulliver, amazed.

The captain and sailorss thought him mad.

Edit this passage from *Dr. Jekyll and Mr. Hyde*.

   Mr Utterson was sitting by his fireside one evening after dinner when he was surprised to receive a visit from Poole.
   "Dear me Poole what brings you here?" he cried.
   Poole looked gloomy. He stood with his shoulders bent and his head hung low.
   What's wrong with you? asked the lawyer.
   "I am very worried about dr. Jekyll," said the butler. "He is shut up again in the laboratory, and I don't like it, sir. I think there's something wrong. Will you come with (I / me) and see for yourself?"
   Mr. Utterson's only answer was to rise and get his hat and coat. A look of relief appeared on Pooles face.
   It was a cold gloomy night in march. Dark clouds raced across the moon as the wind began to rage. Mr. Utterson shivered. Wondered what horror he might find at Dr. Jekyll's.

Edit this passage from *From the Earth to the Moon*.

The cannon that would shoot three mans to the moon had been finished. Michel Ardan the artist and astronaut, wanted some changes made to the space capsule's design. He wanted to (has / have) more room overhead. He felt cramped inside. He felt like a squirrel in a cage He got in touch with the company who builded the capsule and asked them to make a few changes. They said (they / them) would check the design and make the changes.

   Ardan Barbicane and Captain Nicholl were the three astronauts. They waited for all to be ready. The huge silver capsule sparkled in the sunlight.

Expressive Words
Expressive words make writing more exciting.

The words you choose when you write make a big difference. Even a very good story may not turn out very well if it is full of boring words, just as a story that may not seem very good can be made much better by using exciting, expressive words. You can improve your writing by using **exact nouns**, **colorful adjectives**, and **powerful verbs**.

Read the following sentence:

Christine <u>walked</u> into the <u>big</u> <u>building</u>.

If we replace some of the words, will it be better?

Christine <u>marched</u> into the <u>huge</u> <u>skyscraper</u>.

This sentence seems much more exciting than the first one.

Rewrite the sentences replacing nouns, verbs, and adjectives with more exciting, expressive words.

The girl laughed at the funny monkeys.

Casey said, "The grass is getting very long."

My brother says that sports are fun.

The little hamster ate his food.

I picked red flowers to give to my friend.

The rain fell against my window.

Derek ran to the old mailbox.

The blue car drove past our small house.

Edit this passage from *The Pathfinder*.

   Pathfinder decided jasper must talk to Mabel after her father was buried. Mabel was left in Pathfinder's care. It was (his / their) duty to see the girl choose her own happiness.

   On the day they were to leave the island Pathfinder took Mabel and Jasper to a fallen log and told them to sit down. He began by saying that Mabel agreed to be his wife without knowing Jasper's feelings.

   "Pathfinder!" Mabel gasped and turned deathly pale.

   "I've been talking with Jasper. It seems we both (think / thinks) alike when it comes to you."

   Tear after tear runned down the girls cheeks. "I've promised my father..." She bowed her head.

   Mabel's shoulders shook with silent cries. Finally she looked at Jasper to see if all Pathfinder said was true. she saw that it was.

   It was time to go. Pathfinder took Mabel's hands, his eyes wet with tears. "Jasper be happy and take good care of her."

   Pathfinder waved good-bye.

Edit this passage from *The Time Machine*.

    Back through time he flew, until at last he was in (him / his) own laboratory on the same day he had left it. He heard people talking in the next room and knew that we his dinner guests must be there. His feet still sore, he limped in to join us.
    This was the story that our friend the Time Traveller told us as we sat at his dinner table that night. As he'd warned us, it was hard to believe, but how else could we explain his cuts scratches and bloody socks?

    The next morning i went alone to the Time Traveller's house.

    For one second I thought I saw the Time Traveller on his machine but both disappeared like ghosts before my eyes. The laboratory was empty. Eager to see what new story my friend would bring back, I waited as long as I could. He didn't come back. Three years (has / have) passed and he still hasn't returned.

Edit this passage from *Captains Courageous*.

   Several years later, on the West Coast, dan and Harvey met again. Dan was standing in front of the Cheyne's house in california when Harvey rode in on his horse.

  "Hello Dan!"

  "Hello, Harve!"

  "What's the best with you " asked Harvey.

  Dan told Harvey that he (was / were) going to be the second mate on the next trip of a freighter owned by the Cheynes. Harvey told Dan that he was coming into the business for good in the fall and would be taking over the freighters.

  The ex-cook from the *We're Here* comed out to take Harvey's horse.

  Man, he said, pointing to Dan. "Master," he said, as he pointed to Harvey. "Do you remember what i said on the *We're Here*, Dan Troop?" asked the cook

  "It does look like that's the way things are (right / write) now," said Dan.

Edit this passage from *David Copperfield*.

I was gone for months, and before I knew it, a year had passed. Agnes wrote me many letters filled with news about Aunt Betsey Traddles and Micawber. Aunt Betsey was fine and Agnes had helped her plant a garden. Traddles now had his own law business. I had to laugh when I (red / read) that Micawber now worked for Traddles. What a pair these two made! I hoped Traddles would keep Micawber out of trouble.

My writing was going very well, and more and more people knew my name. My storys were being read all over the world now. I thought about how pleased mama and Dora and even Steerforth would be with me. They were gone, as were so many others - Ham the baby and Dora's father. I thought of the peggottys who had moved so far away. I thought of the many troubles I went through while growing up. Now that some time has passed, I (feel / feels) I have changed in some way.

Sentence Combining

Sometimes it is helpful to combine short sentences into one longer sentence.

Instead of using a lot of little short sentences, sometimes you can combine two or more sentences into one. Read through the example below.

I baked some cookies. They were chocolate chip cookies. I baked them for my friend, Anne. She is my best friend.

These four sentences can easily be combined into a single sentence.

I baked some chocolate chip cookies for my best friend, Anne.

Combine each group of sentences below into one sentence.

I like baseball. I like football. I also like volleyball.

She picked out a new watch. It was a black watch. The wristband was made of leather.

The boy went to the pet store. The boy was twelve years old. He went to the pet store to watch the fish.

For supper we are having spaghetti. There is also garlic bread.

The airplane had many seats. The seats were blue. The seats were also striped.

Edit this passage from *Dr. Jekyll and Mr. Hyde.*

As Mr. Utterson read Dr. Lanyon's letter, his heart was beating so fast that he thought it would explode.

(The following is the letter from Dr. Lanyon.)

Midnight had just rung over london when there came a soft knock on my door. I heard the sound of a freight horn. A short man was standing in the shadows.

"Did Dr. Jekyll send you?" I asked. He told me yes, and I bid him enter. When he stepped into the light I must say I was struck by the wild look on his face.

He took the drugs from Dr. Jekylls strange cargo and put them in the glass.

He put the glass to his lips and drank. He cried out staggered and grabbed at the table.

"Oh no!" I screamed again and again, for before my eyes, there stood Henry Jekyll!

I will say but one last thing Utterson and try to believe it. The creature who came to my house that night and turned into Henry Jekyll was none other than Mr. Hyde.

Edit this passage from *Gulliver's Travels*.

A few months after returning to england, Lemuel Gulliver sailed away again. What other wonders would he find across the seas?

What is this place? asked Gulliver.
"Laputa," came the answer.
Gulliver looked around. What a strange place! What strange people Their heads were bent to the right or left. Their clothes were covered with suns moons and stars. They spent all (his / their) time thinking and studying. It seemed they (was / were) only interested in arithmetic and music. Yet all their learning seemed to cause them trouble.

Gulliver left laputa the same way he came, by climbing down a long chain. He found himself in a new country called Balnibarbi.
The Balnibarbians had no common sense. They didnt know a good idea from a bad one. This gulliver learned when he visited the city of Lagado, where a center of learning was opened.
Gulliver was amazed by what he saw (their / there / they're). People were working hard and getting nowhere! Great amounts of money were being spent on all kinds of foolish ideas.

Edit this passage from *From the Earth to the Moon*.

The three astronauts arrived. Addressing the crowd, Michel Ardan said, We are ready to make our way into space!

The crowd roared again as they waved to the crew.

"Thank you all (for / four) coming," added Barbicane. He was pleased at the number of persons who supported (there / their / they're) efforts.

Captain Nicholl the third astronaut was unusually quiet. He looked at the crowd with tears of joy in his eyes. He, like barbicane, was pleased that so many had come to see them off. He was upset that he might never see any of them again.

"You are heroes " the crowd shouted. (They / Them) yelled so loud that the music being played could hardly be heard. The excitement seemed to grow with every passing moment.

The three astronauts stepped into a big, wire cage. Then the door closed.

A loud noise came from below that was louder than any sound ever heard before. The ground shaked like an earthquake as smoke and fire shot out of the ground. Only a few people saw the capsule shoot into the air. It (has / had) happened so fast!

Final Examination

Edit this passage from *Twenty Thousand Leagues Under the Sea*.

Ned rushed into the professor's cabin one day and shouted to him, "We are heading south to Antarctica and the South Pole."

At the south pole, they came upon another adventure with icy waters and whales. There, captain Nemo put up a black flag with an "N" on it. Spoke loudly for all to hear.

"Today, March 21 1868, I Captain Nemo have reached the South Pole. I now claim it as mine."

After a few more adventures the professor and Ned were no longer comfortable being on the *Nautilus*. They realized (them / they) could no longer stay on the ship. They wanted to go home.

Ned and the professor planned their escape right away. They headed for the small boat. They lowered the boat down into the water Freedom was near.

Something happened. The *Nautilus* and the small boat carrying Ned, the professor, and Conseil were caught up in the middle of a whirlpool.

The professor blacked out. The next thing he knew, he Ned and Conseil were in a fisherman's cabin off the coast of norway. He did not know what happened. A miracle maybe - or an act of God? The professor had (no / know) answers.

Complete Sentences

If your students need some additional help with complete sentences, write a few more examples and ask them to point out the two different parts in each sentence. When they understand, have them begin the exercise.

If your students are having trouble with the exercise, have them read each sentence out loud to you and point out both parts of the sentence.

Read the sentences. If they are complete sentences, write a "C" in the blank. If they are not, write an "S" (subject) or a "P" (predicate) to tell which part is there.

Candy is very good. __C__   Had to go home. __P__
That cute little girl. __S__   The gray mouse. __S__
He read the book. __C__   I drew a picture. __C__

Read the run on sentence below and make it into shorter sentences. (Answers may vary.)

I woke up on Saturday morning and remembered I had chores to do. I got dressed as quickly as I could. It was warm outside and I wanted to play. I had to get my chores finished so I could go outside and play with my friends. They were going to go swimming and I wanted to go with them. I love swimming.

If students are having a hard time identifying the sentence fragments in the passage, have them read each sentence out loud. As they read each sentence, have them identify both parts. In this way, they should be able to find the sentence fragments.

That night, Mr. Utterson could not enjoy his meal, for he was worried about his friend Dr. Jekyll. Mr. Enfield's tale of the strange building made him suspect that the doctor was in deep trouble. <u>After dinner, Mr. Utterson.</u> (S) From a safe, he took a sealed envelope that said "Dr. Jekyll's will." Opening it, Mr. Utterson frowned. <u>Had left everything to his partner, Mr. Hyde.</u> (P) The lawyer remembered how he had refused to give the least help to Jekyll in the making of the will. Now that it was made, though, he took charge of it. <u>Had been angered by his lack of knowledge about Mr. Hyde.</u> (P) Now it was what he knew about Hyde that bothered him even more. The lawyer thought the will was madness and had warned Jekyll against it. <u>After hearing Mr. Enfield's horrible tale, Mr. Utterson.</u> (S)

If needed, write more of each type of sentence until students understand the different ending punctuation required for each type.

As mentioned on the student's page, it is sometimes possible to end a sentence more than one way. Usually this only causes confusion between exclamation points or periods, and often either one can be used with only a slight change in meaning. For this reason, it is not "wrong" if students use periods in place of exclamation points or vice versa (unless the sentence obviously requires one or the other). If this happens, simply take the opportunity to discuss both possibilities and decide which would be more effective.

Add capital letters and ending punctuation to the sentences below.

<u>D</u>o you play an instrument<u>?</u>
<u>T</u>here are a lot of people in this world<u>.</u>
<u>T</u>he car went speeding by<u>!</u>   (A period could also be used here.)
<u>H</u>e yelled, "Run<u>!</u>"
<u>I</u>s Erica coming to the party<u>?</u>
<u>R</u>ed apples taste better than green apples<u>.</u>
<u>S</u>uddenly, a light flashed<u>!</u>

Again, if students have a hard time deciding whether to use exclamation points or periods, examine both possibilities.

There are 9 errors in this passage.

"Do you think I *chose* to come aboard your dirty ship<u>?</u> Of course I'm happy about being saved," continued Harvey, "but the sooner you take me to New York, the better you will get paid."

Harvey pushed his hand down into his pants pocket for some money<u>.</u>

"I've been robbed!" he cried. "<u>I</u> had over a hundred dollars. Give it back<u>!</u>"

The look on the man's face changed. His language became strong.

"If I were *you*, I wouldn't call the boat that helped save you any names. I'm Disko Troop of this fishing schooner, *We're Here*. <u>D</u>isko Troop is no thief and neither is any man aboard. I'm sorry about your money, but a boy your age has no business carrying that much<u>.</u> We cannot go back to New York, and we won't be near land until September."

"It's May," shouted Harvey. "I can't wait until *you're* ready<u>!</u> What am I supposed to do in the meantime<u>?</u>"

"Listen to Dan and help him," answered Disko. "He'll teach you about sea life. <u>I</u>'ll pay you ten and a half dollars a month."

91

Review Time!

There are 9 errors in this passage.

The sailing ship was in terrible danger! Strong winds blew it towards the rocks. The sailors and passengers were afraid. What would happen when the ship struck?
One of the passengers, Lemuel Gulliver, was very frightened, but he knew he had to try to save himself.
Crraaa-aack! Was dashed against the rocks and began to break apart. (P) Some of the men jumped into the water, swimming for their very lives. Of them all, only Gulliver reached safety. Climbing out of the water onto the shore of a tiny island, he walked for a while. Then, worn out, he laid down and fell into a deep sleep.
At last Gulliver. (S) He tried to get up, but he found he could not move. What was wrong? He looked down at his body and discovered that he was tied to the ground. It was not rope that held him, but thin cord - a lot of it. Even his hair was fastened to the ground.
Gulliver felt something moving on his leg. He struggled to see and was astonished by what he saw. It was a tiny man less than six inches tall.

Nouns

If students need more help with nouns, think up nouns together until the students are able to easily think of them on their own. Try changing some of the nouns into proper nouns until they understand the difference.

Help students understand that sometimes words like "Mom" and "Dad" may take the place of a name. For example, in the sentence "After supper, Dad washed the dishes," *Dad* is capitalized because it is used for his name - "After supper, Jim washed the dishes." However, in the sentence "After supper, my dad washed the dishes," it is not capitalized because you would not put a name there - "After supper, my Jim washed the dishes."

Also point out that initials are capitalized and that unimportant words in titles are not capitalized (unless they are the first word in the title).

Underline and capitalize all of the proper nouns.
Who is your favorite football team? I like the Green Bay Packers.
She is going to come and visit. She will drive through New York.
My mom went to the store. Denise and Kristen went with her.
Can you run for two miles without stopping?
I wish I had a puppy. My friend has a puppy, Mischief.
I bought a ticket to go and see the movie The Wizard of Oz.
My favorite place to go is Sand Ridge State Park.
There weren't very many people at the recital, but Nancy came.
I grew up in Iowa. I wish that I was from Wisconsin.
The apple tree was planted in the middle of our backyard.

All of the nouns are in red for your benefit, but the student is only asked to circle ten common nouns and underline and capitalize the proper nouns.

The Gun Club was made up of very nice men. Some of these Gun Club members were officers. Then, one day, the shooting slowed. The war was coming to an end. Then it stopped. Members of the Gun Club became very bored. The rooms of their club became empty. Sounds of snoring came from dark corners.
"It's disappointing!" Tom Hunter said one evening. "There's nothing to do! What a weary life!"
"You're right!" spoke Colonel Bloomsberry.
"No war in sight!" said J.T. Maston. He scratched his head. "Only this morning I made a set of plans that will change how wars work!"
"How interesting!" said Tom Hunter. "Maybe we could build weapons for the wars taking place in Europe."
"No," said Maston, "that wouldn't work. It seems that Americans don't want to take action! For example, didn't America once belong to England?"
"Yes," answered Tom.
"Then why shouldn't it be England's turn to belong to America?" said Mason.
The club members argued for a long time.

Capitalization

If students need some extra practice, have them try and list out more words that need capitalized, including titles and names for people. They can also write some sentences that include the word "I."

If they have trouble with the exercise, you may want to write some additional sentences for them to practice with before they move on to a passage.

Write in capital letters where they belong.
Every Thanksgiving, Grandma Gensch comes to visit.
She has a meeting on Wednesday afternoon.
The captain took his orders from General Morgan.
Next fall, I will turn 24 years old.
He got his basketball on Christmas Eve.
Do you think she will work this summer?
I think I will invite Pastor Mike.
The leaves are prettiest in September.
Is Doctor T. Billings open on Saturdays?
I hope I don't get sick at all in March.

92

In this passage, all students have to do is capitalize the words that need to be capitalized. There are no other errors.

There are 8 words that need to be capitalized.

"Jekyll," said Utterson. "You know I am a man to be trusted. Come clean with this matter, and I will help you."

"Utterson," said the doctor, "this is very good of you, but it isn't as bad as you think. The moment I choose, I can be rid of Hyde. Why, I can make him disappear like a magician waving a magic wand."

Utterson thought for a while. "I guess you are right," he said at last, getting to his feet.

"One more thing," continued the doctor. "I really do take great interest in poor Hyde. I want you to promise to carry out the will in his favor should something happen to me."

"I can't say that I will ever like Hyde," said the lawyer, sighing, "but, well, I promise."

Nearly a year later, in the month of October, London was startled by the cruel killing of a highly-respected citizen.

Review Time!

There are 16 words that need to be capitalized.

When Professor Aronnax came to New York, people questioned him. He had written a book called "Mysteries of the Great Submarine Grounds." The professor was famous for being an expert in this field.

More and more people asked the professor for his opinion. He gave them this answer. "The ocean deep is not known to us. We do not know of all the creatures that live there. I can only say that there must be a living creature in the sea that is at the bottom of this. It could be as long as sixty feet. With all its power and strength, the creature is doing much harm in our waters."

The professor's opinion was talked about widely. Because of his knowledge, his opinion was respected by many people.

The United States made plans to send out a large ship to find the creature. It was called the Abraham Lincoln. The Abraham Lincoln had been carefully picked for the voyage. It was a ship of great speed and great strength. The captain of the ship was Commander Farrugut.

Abbreviations

For the purpose of this book, it is simplest for students to think of all abbreviations as being capitalized and marked with periods. However, abbreviations for units of weight and measurement are not, so we can not make this statement. (In fact, the abbreviation for pound, "lb," does not follow any rules.) Emphasize to students that all the abbreviations that they will be working with in this book do require capitalization and periods.

Students may not know all of the abbreviations. Encourage them to write them as well as they can. Make sure they end each abbreviation they write with a period. You may wish to share with students that "May" is the only month for which there is no abbreviation. Although they are very short as well, even "June" and "July" have abbreviations (Jun. and Jul.).

In the sentences below, the underlined words should be abbreviated. Write the abbreviations by the words.

Sometimes it snows a lot in February. (Feb.)
Mister (Mr.) and Misses (Mrs.) S. Cox moved across town.
I have an appointment on Tuesday (Tues.), June (Jun.) 8th.
Are you going to live on Washington Street. (St.)
His father's name was Dean R. Mullins, Senior. (Sr.)
Doctor (Dr.) Rawlins fixed my broken leg.
There should be an extra Friday (Fri.) for every Monday. (Mon.)
Miss (Ms.) Penn took a picture of Riverside Avenue. (Ave.)

All students need to do in this passage is make sure that the proper nouns and abbreviations are capitalized and that the abbreviations have periods. The error number is high because they are easy errors.

There are 18 errors in this passage.

"I must get to the bottom of this!" said Mr. Utterson, as he put on his coat and went out into the icy London night. He headed in the direction of Cavendish Square, where his friend the great Dr. Lanyon had his home. Dr. Lanyon was also an old friend of Dr. Jekyll's. "If anyone knows more about this curious matter, it will be Lanyon," Utterson thought.

"I suppose, Lanyon," said Mr. Utterson, "you and I must be the two oldest friends that Henry Jekyll has."

Dr. Lanyon's face took on a curious appearance. "Yes, I suppose we are. What of it? I see little of him now."

"Indeed?" said Utterson. "I thought you worked together."

"We did," answered Lanyon, "but it is more than ten years since Henry Jekyll has become too mad for me. He began to go wrong, wrong in the mind." Dr. Lanyon shook his head. "Such nonsense in these modern days."

Mr. Utterson decided to ask the question he had come to put. "Did you ever come across a partner of Jekyll's, a Hyde?"

"Hyde?" repeated Dr. Lanyon. "No. Never heard of him."

Plural Nouns

If students need more examples, make a list of plural nouns for each group ("y," "sh," "f," etc.). Try and have students think of several on their own, particularly for irregular plural nouns.

Read the sentences below and write the plural nouns in the blanks.
There was a white house. There were two white ___houses___ .
I used a match to light the fire. I used two _matches_ to light the fire.
We have one library in town. We have two ___libraries___ in town.
A woman was walking by. Two ___women___ were walking by.
Did you see that blue bus? Did you see those two blue _buses_ ?
There was a knife on the table. There were two _knives_ on the table.

When students find misspelled plural nouns in the passages, they are to cross them out and write in the correct word. These are the only errors in this passage.

There are 5 misspelled plural nouns in this passage.

"My good ~~friendes~~ are pleased to help me bring you to your father's fort. Jasper owns a large boat and helps the British move their ~~soldierz~~ from place to place. Big Serpent is a brave and famous chief." Pathfinder pointed to the ~~deers~~ cooking over the fire. "Eat with us. Then we'll start off."

Pathfinder moved to whisper into the ear of Mabel's uncle. "We need your help, sir. The forest is alive with our ~~enemys~~, the Iroquois. Cast your glance into the deep darkness of the forest and let us know if you see something."

Mabel's uncle replied, "Aye. I'll keep a sea watch. Never you fear! I can see a bit of light ~~miless~~ away on the open ocean. I admit, this forest is different, but it's nothing that I can't manage."

Review Time!

There are 10 errors in this passage.

One morning Peggotty said, "Come along now, <u>M</u>aster <u>D</u>avy. You're coming to my house for awhile."

"Mama can't live alone," I told her.

"She's staying with a friend," Peggotty explained<u>.</u> There were ~~teares~~ in Mama's eyes as she waved good-bye. Soon I forgot about Mama and the awful Mr<u>.</u> Murdstone. "Over there is my brother's house," Peggotty said, pointing to a barge by the bay.

"This boat is his house<u>?</u>" I asked. "It's wonderful!" I even liked the fishy smell. Her brother, <u>M</u>r. Peggotty, was a fisherman. <u>Loved all who shared his funny house.</u> (P) With them lived an orphan girl, little <u>E</u>mily, and an orphan boy, Ham. Ham was older than Emily. He was six ~~foots~~ tall, with strong arms used for hard work. Little Emily wore blue beads and had beautiful hair. I could tell that Ham loved Emily.

Verbs

If students need some extra practice with verbs, encourage them to come up with several verbs of each type. To make it easier, you could write sentences leaving blanks for verbs and let the students fill them in.

On the other hand, if the exercise seems easy for students, you may want to go an extra step and have them identify each verb in the exercise as an action, linking, or helping verb.

Read the sentences below and circle all of the verbs.
The boy *climbed* up the ladder.   (action)
Coleen *was* excited.   (linking)
The horse *ran* through the stable.   (action)
They *are bringing* dessert.   (helping, action)
Miles *listened* to the crickets.   (action)
We *will find* the perfect present.   (helping, action)

Students are asked to edit this passage and circle as many verbs as they can find, including at least two linking verbs, three helping verbs, and three action verbs.

There are 2 errors and one misspelled plural noun in this passage.

The man, armed with a bow and arrow, was (h) walking (a) on Gulliver's leg. He was (h) followed (a) by many others just like him. Startled, Gulliver cried (a) out.

The band of tiny men jumped (a) off his body in a hurry. To them, Gulliver was (l) a giant and his cry of surprise was (l) a roar. Gulliver struggled (a) against the cords. He was (h) able (a) to free his left arm. At this, shouts of alarm rose (a) around him. Hundreds of tiny ~~bowss~~ were (h) raised (a). Gulliver was (h) showered (a) with arrows. They felt (l) like needles in the skin of his arm.

Gulliver lay (a) back, his arm hurting (a) terribly. He would (h) do (a) nothing more to frighten the little folk around him. He waited (a) quietly.

17

Verb Tenses

If your students need some additional help with verb tenses, try an exercise where they change the same verb into different tenses. For example, use the framework "Today she _____ ; yesterday she _____ ; tomorrow she _____ ." Then pick a simple verb like "walk" and have students fill in the blanks. "Today she walks; yesterday she walked; tomorrow she will walk." Let them practice with several different verbs before they move on to the exercise.

Write the tense of the underlined verbs in the blanks provided.

He ate his lunch.	past
The monkey is sleeping.	present
Arthur will play tomorrow.	future
The woman shall walk her dog.	future
The bird sang a song.	past
Diane is sick.	present
I looked at my watch.	past
Those boys will be at the movie.	future

18

Most of the verbs in this passage will be in past tense because the story is told in this tense. However, some of the verbs are in future tense and present tense. If you would like to give your students extra practice, pick some of the verbs and have them write or say them in a different tense.

Circle as many verbs as you can find and identify the verb tense.

"I have invented (past) a machine that I think (present) will travel (future) through time," our friend told (past) us. At first, no one said (past) anything. Our friend liked (past) to make jokes, but tonight he looked (past) very serious. It was (past) also true that he was (past) an inventor. Even the chairs we were sitting (past) in were (past) not ordinary chairs, but his own special design.

Then one of the other guests laughed. (past) "Travel (present) through time?" he chuckled. (past) "That is (present) not possible."

"That is (present) what everyone thinks (present)," our friend replied, nodding (past). "Perhaps that is (present) why no one has (past) ever bothered (past) to try."

There was (past) more laughter.

"If you do not believe (present) me," our friend said, (past) "I guess (present) I will have (future) to show you."

"Here," our friend answered. (past) Looking (present) closely, we saw (past) that his hands did contain (past) a small metal object. He explained (past) that it was (past) just a model of the machine he had talked (past) about, but it would really work. (future)

19

Review Time!

In this passage students must correct the errors as well as find two past tense, two present tense, and two future tense verbs.

There are 5 errors in this passage.

Three hours before the Abraham Lincoln was (past) to set sail, Professor Aronnax received (past) a letter. It was worded (past) as follows:

> Sir:
> Will you join (future) the Abraham Lincoln in our search for the great creature? The government of the United States will be (future) happy to have you on our voyage. A cabin will be (future) ready for you.

Up until he received (past) the letter, Professor Aronnax longed (past) to go home to France. He wanted (past) to see his home, his country, and his friends. After reading (present) the letter, all Professor Aronnax could think (past) about was finding (past) the sea creature. Finding (present) it was (past) to become his biggest wish in life.

20

95

Irregular Verbs

Students probably know and use most irregular verbs already. However, some of them might be a little tricky. To familiarize students with irregular verbs, use the same framework you used when introducing verb tense, only with irregular verbs. For example, with the irregular verb "swim," the student would say "Today they <u>swim</u>; yesterday they <u>swam</u>."

Fill in the blanks with the past tense of the verbs in parentheses.
A butterfly (fly) ____flew____ by my window yesterday.
My uncle (give) ____gave____ me a big hug.
(Do) ____Did____ you see the newspaper today?
The women (speak) ____spoke____ quietly while the baby slept.
Dory (write) ____wrote____ her name at the top of the page.
The little girls (sing) ____sang____ very loudly.
The chickens (eat) ____ate____ all of their feed.
I (give) ____gave____ Mitch a high five as he (run) ____ran____ by.
They (are) ____were____ tired until they (take) ____took____ their naps.

There are 4 errors and 6 incorrect irregular verbs in this passage.

The very next day, each member of the club received the following message:

Baltimore, October

The president of the Gun Club has the honor of telling his friends that during the meeting on <u>O</u>ctober 5, he will make an announcement that they will be very interested in. He insists that they all be at the meeting.

Impey <u>B</u>arbicane, President

October 5th comed (came). All the members crowded into a hall. It was a big meeting. Models of cannons, rifles, and other war weapons filled the hall. A huge iron desk ised (was) at the far end of the room. Behind it sitted (sat) the president of the club, <u>I</u>mpey Barbicane. The club members knowed (knew) he would not have insisted they be there unless it was very important.

Impey Barbicane was a quiet, cold, serious man<u>.</u> He was a true Yankee. He had maked (made) a fortune in the lumber business. He standed (stood) out from the other men.

Contractions

If students are having trouble understanding the formation of contractions, continue to list word pairs that can be made into contractions. Then show which letters are taken out and how the apostrophe fits into the space.

There is one exclusion to this standard, which is "won't." Write it out for the students and show them the two words that form it, "will" and "not." Point out the "o," which is not in the word "will," but is included in the contraction.

If students have trouble with the exercise, remind them to look over their list of common words and pronouns in contractions. Then they can look specifically for these words in the sentences.

Circle the pairs of words that can be made into contractions. Write the contractions in the blanks provided.
It was not a dangerous dinosaur. ____wasn't____
I will take off my shoes before I enter. ____I'll____
She promised that she would read my favorite book. ____she'd____
Do you know if they are happy? ____they're____
Ian did not think it was cold outside. ____didn't____
The snow blew harder than I had ever seen it blow. ____I'd____
This is not what I had in mind. ____isn't____
Do you think it is a good idea? ____it's____
Liz thought he had gone to the store. ____he'd____

There are 4 errors, 1 incorrect irregular verb, and 10 pairs of words that can be made into contractions in this passage.

"My friends, we have (we've) been at peace for too long a period! We must take action! Any war that would (that'd) bring back the use of weapons would be welcome!" speaked (spoke) Barbicane.

The members yelled in support.

Barbicane continued, "For now, war is not (isn't) possible. We must accept this and find another way to use our energy. For a long time I have (I've) been thinking of a plan. <u>T</u>his plan will make a great noise in the world."

"A great noise?" the colonel asked with great excitement.

"You have (You've) all seen the moon, have not (haven't) you?" <u>B</u>arbicane asked. "Well, I will (I'll) lead you weary men on an adventure. An adventure to the moon<u>!</u>"

The crowd cheered! Each member of the club was excited by Barbicane's words.

The voices died down. Barbicane spoke again, this time in a deeper voice. "You all know how firearms have improved these last few years. With this in mind, <u>I</u> started to wonder if it would (it'd) be possible to build a huge cannon. A cannon large enough to shoot something to the moon. I have (I've) looked at it carefully. I think we can succeed! My good friends, let us (let's) do it!"

Review Time!

There are 4 errors, 5 incorrect irregular verbs, and 7 pairs of words that can be made into contractions.

Harvey entered Disko's cabin and standed (stood) before the captain. "I have not (I've or haven't) acted quite right, and I am (I'm) here to say I am (I'm) sorry," said Harvey, surprised at his own quiet tone.

Disko standed (stood) up and holded (held) out the largest hand Harvey had ever seen. "You will (You'll) make a man yet if you go on this way," said Disko.

Disko shaked (shook) Harvey's hand, cutting off the feeling halfway up Harvey's arm. "Go about your business now," said Disko.

Harvey maked (made) his way to the deck to see Dan.

"Well, I am (I'm) glad that is settled," said Dan, "but you have (you've) got a lot to learn." Dan began to show Harvey the parts of the schooner.

"Guess I have," said Harvey, as he stared out thoughtfully over the shining sea.

25

Pronouns

If students are unsure about how to use pronouns, write more pairs of sentences in which the first uses a noun and the second replaces it with a pronoun. Write some sentences using subjective pronouns and some using objective pronouns to make sure they understand the difference. When they are ready, have them begin the exercise.

Choose the correct pronouns in the sentences below.
After the meeting, (they/them) drove home. I went with (they/them).
(We/Us) went on vacation. The hotel gave (we/us) reservations.
(Her/She) made some chocolate candy. It took (her/she) all day.
No one can help (I/me) set the table. (I/Me) will do it by myself.

26

Please note that choosing the correct pronoun does not count as an error.

There are 4 errors and 2 incorrect irregular verbs.

The group canoed down the river until (they/them) saw Big Serpent waving on the shore. Pathfinder steered toward (he/him). Big Serpent had seen fresh tracks of the Iroquois.

At once, Pathfinder taked (took) charge. "Jasper, (you/they) go up river and set a campfire. (They/Them) will think we've made camp there. Big Serpent, you go back into the woods. Watch what happens. I'll take Mabel and the others downstream to that little beach. Do you know where (me/I) mean?"

The young man and Indian nodded. (They/Them) took off in different directions.

Pathfinder and Arrowhead guided the two canoes to the beach. They cut tree branches and bushes to make a cover for everyone to crouch under. Soon, Jasper and Big Serpent joined (they/them) under the leafy tent. Just then, three Iroquois walked onto the beach.

As the three Iroquois comed (came) near to where they hid, Pathfinder and Jasper heard them speak. They were planning to capture Mabel. (Her/She) would become an Indian's wife!

27

Possessives

Possessives ending with an "s" can be tricky. The guidelines given to students are given to simplify the rules. In some cases, it is optional. For example, if a singular noun ends with an "s" or a "z" sound, you may just add an apostrophe. However, there is an exception. If a singular noun ending with "s" is a one syllable word, it requires both an apostrophe and an "s."

For example: **Gus's dog wanted to go for a walk.**

If students need more practice with possessives, write some sentences together that show possession. Make sure that you use possessives like all four of the kinds shown on the page.

If students have no problems with possessives, you may ask them to give possessive nouns and possessive pronouns for each sentence below.

Write a possessive noun or pronoun in the blanks provided.
That computer belongs to my dad. It is __my dad's , his__ computer.
This pizza belongs to that family. It is __that family's , their__ pizza.
That chair belongs to me. It is __my__ chair.
This candy belongs to Mindy. It is __Mindy's , her__ candy.
That plant was given to Alice. It is __Alice's , her__ plant.
This bunk bed belongs to my brothers. It is __my brothers' , their__ bed.
The shelf belongs to Wes. It is __Wes's__ shelf.

28

97

There are 5 errors in this passage.

"Scotland Yard," said the officer. "(We/Us) wish to see Mr. Hyde's rooms."

One could see it was a thrill for the woman to hear this. "Ah," she muttered, "he is in trouble."

The men found Hyde's place torn apart. Clothes were thrown about, and coins were scattered on the floor. Some papers had been burned. From the ashes, the officer pulled part of a check book. The other half of the cane was found behind the door.

The officer was thrilled. "Hyde is in our hands now!" he shouted. "He has money in the bank. All we must do is wait for (he/him) to cash a check!"

This was not to happen. Utterson remembered Jekyll's words. "Perhaps," thinked (thought) the lawyer, "the magician had waved his magic wand."

29

Review Time!

There are 4 errors in this passage.

He let us look at the model as long as (we/us) wished. Then he told us to watch carefully. Setting the tiny machine on the table, he asked one of our friends to push the bar he had shown us before. The Time Traveller taked (took) the guest's hand. The inventor did not have time to coax and tug at the surprised man.

At last the guest touched his finger to the shiny bar. For one second, the machine trembled as if (they/it) were about to do a somersault. Then, right before our eyes, right beneath his shaking hand, the Time Machine disappeared!

"On this machine," our friend said quietly, "I will explore time. I was never more serious in my life."

There was a long silence. I was not at all sure what I thought.

The next week we went to our friend's house again for dinner. There we finded (found) a note from (he/him) saying that he had gone out.

30

Adjectives

If students have any trouble with adjectives, make a list of adjectives together. Make sure to list adjectives that tell how many, what size, what color, how it looks, and how it feels. Have them try to come up with unusual adjectives.

Irregular adjectives include good, better, and best; bad, worse, and worst; and many, more, and most.

You may wish to point out to students that adjectives can come after the subject, although they usually come before.

Circle all of the adjectives in the sentences below.
The little mouse scurried through a tiny hole in the old barn.
That nice, ripe tomato is bigger than an apple!
Those three houses were very neat and clean.
I know this trip was a bad one, but was it the worst trip you've been on?

31

Students are asked only to find as many adjectives as they can. If they miss a lot, you may have them read through the passage a few times, looking for just one type of adjective at a time (descriptive, demonstrative, comparative/superlative, articles).

There are no errors in this passage.

Captain Farragut was a good sea captain. His ship and he were one. The monster responsible for terror on the high seas put Captain Farragut into action. He promised to rid the waters of the great monster.

The officers and crew on the Abraham Lincoln shared the same opinion as the captain. They wanted to meet up with the monster. They would catch up with it and bring it on board. Then they would cut it up. This was the object of the voyage.

Captain Farragut offered two thousand dollars to the first man to spot the monster. Everything needed to catch it was on board.

Captain Farragut had the good sense to have Ned Land, "King of the Harpooners," come along on the trip. Ned was from Canada. He was a large man of great strength. Ned had a no-nonsense manner about him. He did not believe that there was a living creature that was trying to destroy ships at sea.

32

98

Adverbs

If students need extra practice with adverbs, write some sentences and have them add adverbs to them. For example, you might write "The hungry cow ate." Then have them add adverbs. "The (really, very) hungry cow (always, never, barely) ate (sloppily, greedily, much, often)."

It is very important that students understand that "not" is an adverb because it is very common and is often buried in a contraction.

Circle the adverbs in the sentences below.

The grizzly bear growled loudly at the cold wind.
His sister rarely went to the movies.
The caterpillar inched upwards.
I did not step inside the door.
The flowers will be blooming very shortly.
He rode the bus daily.

Students are asked only to find as many adverbs as they can and at least five adjectives. There are no errors in this passage.

My two-week visit with Peggotty passed quickly. "I don't want to leave," I cried, with a shiver. I thought of Mr. Murdstone's mean face.

"It is time," Peggotty said, "so don't be a baby."

"I'll miss you," I told Emily. We waved to each other as the carriage headed toward the Rookery.

At home again, a strange servant greeted us. I cried, "Where's Mama?" Something was terribly wrong; I could feel it! My legs began to shake, and I cried, "Has Mama died?"

"Quiet," Peggotty said, adding seriously, "your mother has remarried." Then Mama's arms were around me, and I hugged her very hard.

"Clara," said Mr. Murdstone, "now don't forget. Boys need a strong hand." I felt Mama shiver as she showed me to my new room.

Review Time!

There are no errors in this passage. Students are asked to underline the possessive nouns and pronouns and circle three adverbs and five adjectives.

A man wearing robes and a crown came. He stood on a stage the little men had built near Gulliver's head.

"I am Golbasto Gue, mighty king of Lilliput. You have entered my kingdom," he shouted.

"My name is Lemuel Gulliver," said Gulliver. He spoke softly so that he would not hurt the king's ears. "I am a poor traveler from England. My ship has crashed on the rocks, and I fear that all on board her have died. Please bring me food. I am very hungry."

The king called for food.

The people brought barrels of drink and baskets of meat and bread. These they emptied into Gulliver's mouth. He ate and drank all of it and asked for more.

Once again, Gulliver fell into a deep sleep.

Subject / Verb Agreement

If students need some extra help with subject / verb agreement, write sentences in present tense alternating between singular and plural subjects, and have students fill in the verbs.

It may be confusing that the singular subjects "I" and "you" agree with plural verbs. If so, make sure that you use "you" and "I" as subjects in some of the sentences you write.

The forms of the verb "to be" are even more confusing in both present and past tense. While students will probably be familiar with them, you may want to give them a list if they are not.

She / He IS	I AM	You ARE	They ARE
She / He WAS	I WAS	You WERE	They WERE
She / He DOES	They / I / You DO		
She / He HAS	They / I / You HAVE		

Choose the correct verb in the sentences below.

Denise (hold/holds) the record for the long jump.
They (am/are) going hiking tomorrow.
Sam and Charlie (play/plays) chess a lot.
I (run/runs) a mile every day.
Will you (mop/mops) the floors after the restaurant closes?
The cats (purr/purrs) whenever you pet them.

99

Choosing the correct verb does not count as an error.

There are 6 errors in this passage.

The sea was very rough, and he (Harvey) wondered why he was not ill. He asked Manuel how much longer the weather would last.
"Maybe two days, maybe more," said Manuel, winking at Harvey.
Harvey smiled weakly. "A week ago I would have been very sick," he said.
"Well, you are a fisherman now," said Manuel.
Fishermen (love/loves) the kind of long talks during which they can (tell/tells) stories and sing sea songs. The talk soon (turn/turns) to shouting, and no one (prove/proves) anything in the end. It was just this kind of talk that Harvey heard on the *We're Here*. Dan beginned (began) with the first two lines of a cheerful rhyme, and one by one, each man joined in, adding to the story. Harvey sitted (sat) back and gave his full attention to the mans. Soon their songs made him forget everything but the sea.

37

Subject / Pronoun Agreement

If students need additional practice with subject / pronoun agreement, write some more sentence like those in the exercise until they are comfortable replacing nouns with pronouns.

Choose the correct pronouns in the sentences below.
Do you like **spinach**? (She/It) is good for you.
I watched the little **boys** play. I had to watch (them/him) closely.
The **butterfly** flew across the meadow. (It/They) was beautiful.
The **woman** walked to the **store**. (Him/She) went inside (them/it).
You should put your **coat** on. (It/He) will keep you warm and cozy.
The **man** took out his **keys**. (He/She) needed (it/them).
Those **kids** caught that **fish**. (He/They) caught (he/it) in the stream.

38

There are 6 errors in this passage.

The same night Barbicane announced his plan, the telegraph wires sent messages to distant places around the country. The whole country swelled with pride.
The next day, over 1,500 newspapers carried news of the plan. Persons wondered if the moon was a complete planet; if (they/it) was changing at all. Was it like the earth had been before people lived there? What did the side that couldn't be seen from the earth look like? All that had been planned so far was to send something to the moon. Every newspaper saw this as the start of many experiments. They hoped someday the earth would unlock the last secrets of the moon's world.

Next, preparation began for the big event. First, Barbicane called members of the Gun Club together. (She/They) agreed to talk with some astronomers. Together, (they/he) worked out the finishing touches of the plan.

39

Review Time!

There are 6 errors in this passage.

The professor (were/was) excited at finding the monster and happy to be saved at the same time. His strength was just about to run out when Conseil came along and saved him.
Conseil helped Professor Aronnax swim to the "floating island." Another hand reached out to help (it/them). To their surprise, it was Ned Land. Had he also been thrown overboard?
(Them/They) soon discovered that the island was made of steel. The monster they had been searching for was made of hard-plate steel! The professor was excited and curious at the same time. (He/They) was happy they had continued on in their search for the monster.
"I have been on this monster for three hours. I have seen no sign of life," said Ned. "Let us explore together," he added. The three men beginned (began) to explore the surface of the steel monster.

100

40

Editing

There are 8 errors in this passage.

It was late in the afternoon when Mr. Utterson found his way to Jekyll's door. He was let in by Poole, the butler, and led across a yard to the laboratory. It was the first time Mr. Utterson had been in that part of the doctor's house, so he looked at everything with great interest.

A fire burned in the fireplace. Close to the warmth sitted (sat) Dr. Jekyll, looking deathly sick. (They/He) did not rise to greet his visitor, but he held out a cold hand and welcomed him in a changed voice.

"(Has/Have) you heard about the killing?" asked Mr. Utterson.

The doctor shivered. "(They/It) were shouting the news in the street," he said.

"One word," said the lawyer. "Carew was my friend, but so are you, and I want you to know what I am doing. Are you responsible for hiding this fellow?"

The doctor raised his handes as if to cover his face.

"Utterson, I promise you," cried Jekyll. "I (gives/give) you my word that I am done with him in this world. He is safe and will never more be heard of."

Editing

There are 7 errors in this passage.

Knowing that the Indians could strike at any moment, Jasper keeped (kept) thinking about Mabel's safety. He jumped at every noise from the forest. They paddled quietly, as the tiniest sound could warn the Iroquois of their whereabouts.

Mabel's heart beat quicker, but (they/she) was not afraid. Her fine blue eyes shone with excitement. She felt ready for whatever would come.

"Mabel!" whispered Jasper, "have no fear for I... we will protect you."

"I am a soldier's daughter! I would be ashamed to say I was afraid."

"Yes, I (know/knows), but also know we will do everything to keep you from harm."

"I believe you. Jasper, don't worry about my fears. I would never stand in the way of your duty."

"Ah, the child is worthy of being a sergeant's daughter," whispered Pathfinder. "Pretty one, your father and I fighted (fought) together many times."

Editing

There are 5 errors in this passage.

As a joke, I said maybe our friend had climbed on his machine, fastened the strap, and gone for a trip through time. One of the guests (was/were) new this week, so we had to explain about the Time Machine. Just as we were telling how the model had seemed about to make a somersault, there was a sound at the door.

In came our friend with his clothess all dirty and torn. He had cuts on his face and walked with a limp. On his feet (he/him) wore only a pair of torn and bloody socks. At first he didn't seem able to speak. He had to tug at my sleeve and point to a glass of water to show that he wanted some. Then he seemed to feel a little better and even smiled.

"What's wrong?" we all asked. "Where (have/has) you been?"

He said he was very hungry and would explain everything after we'd eaten.

"Have you been time travelling?" I cried. "Please (tell/tells) us."

"Yes," he answered, and began to eat.

Editing

There are 7 errors in this passage.

Then came a whisper at the door. "Peggotty?" I asked.

"Davy," she said, "be as quiet as a mouse, or the cat will hear!" I knew she meant Mr. Murdstone.

"How's Mama?" I asked.

Peggotty cried softly. "You'll see her tomorrow... before you go away."

I stood frozen for a moment. "*Away*?" I asked, my heart beating wildly.

"Yes," Peggotty replied, "to a London school."

Her words hit me like a hammer. (Me/I) would be leaving the Rookery. My tears began to fall.

Afraid about what lay ahead, I left for school in the morning. I held tight the cake, money, and the note from Mama. Our servant Peggotty had given it to me. At nine years old, I worried about meeting the head professor and the other boys. I was right to have worried. The professor telled (told) everyone I was to blame for hurting Mr. Murdstone.

Midterm

There are 10 errors in this passage.

    <u>S</u>ome people believed that the moon (was/were) once a comet. A few people believed the moon had passed too closely to the earth and had been catched (caught) by our gravity. Others believed the moon was coming closer every time it went around the earth. (Them/They) thought (he/it) would one day fall against the earth. Finally, people read enough to know that they were wrong<u>.</u>

    Impey <u>B</u>arbicane chose a committee from the members to help him carry out his plan. These members (was/were) as follows: Barbicane himself, General Morgan, <u>M</u>ajor Elphiston, and J<u>.</u>T<u>.</u> Maston. On <u>O</u>ctober 8 they met at Barbicane's house. He spoke first.

    "Gentlemen, we must clear up an important problem. (We/They) must first think about what kind of rocket our cannon will send to the moon<u>.</u>"

Prepositions

    Point out to students the nouns or pronouns that end each prepositional phrase. If students need some extra help identifying prepositions, try writing sentences containing prepositional phrases and then have the students find them. It may help them to identify other parts of the sentence first, such as the subject and verb. When they are able to find the prepositions and prepositional phrases, have them work through the exercise.

Circle the prepositions and underline the prepositional phrases.

I laughed at <u>the clown.</u>
My father was standing by <u>the door.</u>
The trash can is inside <u>the cabinet</u> under <u>the sink.</u>
The kittens stayed in <u>the barn</u> during <u>the storm.</u>
The boy mowed carefully around <u>the rose bushes.</u>
She looked across <u>the street.</u>

Students are asked to circle at least seven prepositions and underline the prepositional phrases. There are no errors in this passage.

    Finally, Jasper returned with <u>Big Serpent</u> riding in <u>the canoe.</u> Big Serpent told them he'd won the battle with <u>the Indian</u> in <u>the river.</u> Then, he crept back to <u>the Iroquois' camp</u> and discovered that Arrowhead was the Iroquois' friend. Arrowhead was telling the Iroquois all of <u>Pathfinder's plans.</u>

    Pathfinder shook his head. "That's why he left me! There is no time to lose. We must get Mabel to <u>the fort.</u> The fastest way is down <u>the Oswego Falls.</u> The Iroquois would never think we'd chance it."

    He looked at <u>Mabel</u> and said gently, "Jasper is an expert in <u>these waters</u>, and it will be best if you went in <u>his canoe.</u> Big Serpent will come with <u>me.</u>"

    Mabel's cheeks grew warm as she moved to <u>handsome Jasper's canoe.</u> The canoe swept along in <u>the dark</u>, and the sound of <u>the falls</u> grew louder and louder.

    Jasper spoke into <u>her ear</u> over <u>the noise.</u> "We are here at <u>the falls.</u> I beg you to trust me. We are not old friends, but I feel I have known you for <u>years.</u>"

    "I feel the same, Jasper, and I do trust you."

Commas

    If students need extra practice, have them write a short letter using commas where necessary. You may want to emphasize to students that while in a friendly letter only the first and last word of the greeting are capitalized, in a business letter all of the important words are capitalized.

Edit this letter by adding capital letters and commas.

                                         <u>J</u>uly 9<u>,</u> 1992

<u>D</u>ear <u>J</u>anine<u>,</u>

    <u>I</u> am sorry that <u>I</u> couldn't come over and play today. <u>I</u> was in <u>D</u>enver<u>,</u> <u>C</u>olorado. <u>I</u>s it okay if <u>I</u> come <u>A</u>ugust 2nd<u>,</u> 1995? <u>T</u>hat is in only 1<u>,</u>119 days. <u>P</u>lease call and let me know if this will work for you.

              <u>L</u>ove<u>,</u>
               <u>R</u>ay

There are 22 errors in this letter.

October 21, 1867

Dear Aunt Ruth,

   Hello! How are you doing? I am doing well. So far our adventure has been dull. We have been at sea for three long months - that's over 2,000 hours - with no sighting of the monster. I still am not at all certain what we should be looking for. The captain says we will turn around soon if we do not see anything.

   I miss everyone back home in Paris, France. It is not the same in the United States, although I did very much enjoy New York City, New York. It is a very nice city. I will be home sometime in the next year. I will see you then!

        Sincerely,
           Professor Aronnax

Review Time!

There are 17 errors in this passage. Students are also asked to underline at last three prepositional phrases, circling the preposition.

   There were many questions. The Gun Club mailed a letter to the famous observatory at Cambridge, Massachusetts. The astronomers and scientists there were known around the world. They also had a very powerful telescope. Two days later, the Gun Club received their answer.

                          Cambridge, Massachusetts
Mr. Impey Barbicane   October 7
President of the Gun Club
Baltimore, Maryland

Dear Mr. Barbicane,
   After receiving your letter, our staff met right away. We answered your questions the best we could.
   The members of the Gun Club must start preparation right away for the launch. If you miss the date, you will not find the moon in the same spot for eighteen more years!
   We at the observatory are ready to help if you have any more questions. We wish you well. You are all the pride of America!

        Sincerely,
           J.M. Belfast

Commas

If students need more practice with commas, have them try to write some sentences like those shown as examples.

For the first rule, using commas in a series, students are taught to use commas after the first two items. However, students may notice some writers omit the comma after the second item in the series (before "and"). This is not technically wrong, but it is becoming more and more common to use a comma here and it helps make the sentence clearer, so it is a good habit for students to get into. Emphasize to students that commas are not needed if all of the words in a series are connected by the word "and" - for example:

      I like penguins <u>and</u> chopsticks <u>and</u> ponytails.

You may choose to discuss the second rule in more depth. Tell students that these introductory phrases could not stand alone, they are dependent clauses. If you took them away, you would still be left with the main part of a sentence.

Add commas where they belong in the sentences below.
The baby smiled, laughed, and rolled over.
Were you scared by that loud, shrill whistle?
When the girls woke up, they made breakfast.
Polly asked for two long ribbons.

There are 7 errors in this passage.

   The professor, Conseil, and Ned walked about hoping to find some signs of life on the floating island. Some time had gone by when they felt a sudden motion. The monster began to move slowly through the icy waters.

   It was a long night for the three of them. They held on tightly to the monster for fear of being thrown into the sea. All they could do was hold on tight and wait. The motion did not stop. Their only hope was that the monster would not go beneath the surface of the water. It was a very long, cold night for them.

   Morning came. All of a sudden the motion of the steel monster came to a stop. Some kind of iron plate, like a door, seemed to open up right where they were standing. Eight men of great strength dragged them down into the monster.

   Ned, Conseil, and the professor spent much time sleeping. After they woke, they spent a good deal of time talking. Ned became angry.

   Professor Aronnax, being a patient man, kept Ned from going into a rage. While the professor was upset, he knew it would be dangerous to do something foolish.

103

Commas

If students need extra practice with commas, you may want to have them write several sentence like those used as examples. Have them write at least a couple sentences for each rule covered on the page.

Point out to students that when they add commas for direct address, people may not always be addressed by name (as shown in the last sample sentence).

Add commas to the sentences below.
There are, I believe, more cookies in the pantry.
Do you want to go skating, Marsha, or skiing?
Oh, that would be nice.
Cara, this shirt is for you.
Hey, you can't go in there!

There are 5 errors in this passage.

"I cannot tell you how I know this, but I am sure he will never return," said Jekyll. "There is one thing I would like to ask you, Utterson. I have received a letter from Hyde, and I don't know if I should show it to the police. I should like to leave it in your hands and have you decide."

The letter was signed by Edward Hyde. It said that he was grateful for all of Dr. Jekyll's help, but it would no longer be necessary for the doctor to worry about him. He had a way to escape and would bother no one again.

"Well, you have had a fine escape," continued Utterson. "I'm sure Hyde wanted to kill you and collect the money."
"Oh, more than that," moaned Jekyll, "I have learned something which I shall never forget."
On his way out, Utterson stopped to exchange a word with Poole.
"By the way, Poole," he said. "A letter was delivered by hand today. Who brought it?"
Poole was sure that nothing had come except by mail.

Review Time!

There are 10 errors in this passage.

In Blefuscu, Gulliver was not so comfortable. There was no chair, bed, or table. He had no cooks to supply his food. Life in Blefuscu would be harder than it had been in Lilliput.

One day, Gulliver was walking along the shore. He saw something large and dark in the water. The rising tide brought it nearer. He saw that it was an empty boat. Not just an empty boat, but a boat his size!

Diving into the water, he swam to the boat and fastened the rope to it. He began to swim for land. It was slow, but the boat was moving toward land. Some Blefuscudian ships joined him, fastening lines to the boat too. Slowly, they approached the beach. At last, the boat was on dry land!

It took a month, but at last the boat was ready. Gulliver was on his way home!

Back home, Gulliver showed off his tiny animals, charging people to see them, and he made a great deal of money. He was not happy, for he longed for excitement. He sold his sheep and cattle. He left the money for his wife and children and, once again, he set out on a ship on a search for adventure.

Commas

If students need more practice with these rules, write some more sentences following the examples and then have them try and write some.

It can be tricky for them to remember when to use a comma with a conjunction. Just remind them to stop when they read one of these words (AND, BUT, OR, FOR, NOR, SO, or YET) and check to see if there is a complete sentence on both sides. If there is, a comma is needed.

Add commas where they belong in the sentences below.
She wanted to go to the store and to the bank.
You can have your supper now, or you can have it later.
My father, that man by the door, is always early.
It does not seem very late, yet the sun has been down for hours.
Geeves, the butler, answered the door, but there was no one there.

There are 9 errors in this passage.

Summer passed, and when fall came I was allowed a visit to the Rookery. I noticed that Mama seemed ill, and she spoke slowly, having to pause often. Her husband, Mr. Murdstone, made my holiday a bad one, ordering me to stay away from Peggotty.

"So, this is Davy!" I heard someone say. I looked up to see a jolly man coming toward me. "I'm Mr. Micawber," he said, as he reached to shake my hand, "and you're going to live with me and my family."

I soon came to learn that the Micawbers could not pay their bills even though Mr. Murdstone sent them money for taking me in. As the weeks passed, I offered to share my work money with them.

"We couldn't take your money, Davy," Mrs. Micawber said. "You need that money for your food and clothes, but you can help."

I helped them get money in that way, but it didn't take care of their problems.

57

Semi-Colons

If students need more help with semi-colons, write a few more sentences like those used in the example to help them understand that when there is no conjunction, a semi-colon is used rather than a comma. It may help if you write sentences with commas and conjunctions, and then have them rewrite the sentences without the conjunctions and replace the commas with semi-colons. Emphasize that if they do see a conjunction (AND, BUT, YET, FOR, OR, SO, or NOR) then they will not need a semi-colon.

Again, note that semi-colons are used to join independent clauses.

Add semi-colons where they belong in the sentences below.

There is a robin in the tree; it looks lonely.
Max wants to watch a movie and then go to bed.
The man opened his umbrella; it was raining outside.
Kim said she would watch her sister; her mother is sick.
The queen ordered the seamstress to make her dress; the baker to bake some pies, cookies, and bread; and the maid to polish her crown.

58

There are 8 errors in this passage.

That night, the fog rolled over the streets and wrapped the city in silence. Mr. Utterson and Mr. Guest sat in the lawyer's study enjoying some wine.

Utterson handed Guest the letter. Guest's eyes grew bright as he studied it with great interest.

"No, sir," he said. "He's not mad, but it is a strange hand."

Just then, a servant entered with a note from Dr. Jekyll. "Ah," said Utterson, "Jekyll is inviting me to dinner."

Mr. Guest was familiar with Dr. Jekyll's handwriting after his many years of service to Mr. Utterson. "Could I see the note?" asked Guest.

He put the papers next to each other and looked at them closely. "The two hands are equal in many points; they are only differently sloped," he decided.

Guest and Utterson exchanged silent glances. "I would not speak of this note, you know," said the master.

"No, sir," said the clerk in an equally serious voice.

That night, Mr. Utterson locked the note in his safe.

59

Review Time!

There are 9 errors in this passage.

At last our friend pushed his plate away and looked around at us. Now he was ready to tell the whole story.

That very morning, he said, he put the final touches on the Time Machine.

He took a deep breath and a strong grip on the bar, and so began his journey into time.

As he watched the world flash white with snow and green with grass, he knew he must be travelling almost a year a second. Still he travelled on and on. At last he decided he was ready to stop. Taking hold of the bar which turned off the machine, he went head over heels. It was lucky our friend the Time Traveller was tough, for he was quite shaken by the fall. He found himself on a soft green lawn with the Time Machine lying on its side near him. A huge white statue stood close by. It looked like an enormous, ugly bird with a cruel smile.

Then he heard someone coming. He wondered if it was a party of scouts sent to find out what or who he was. He feared they might try to capture or harm him. As soon as he saw them, his fears were at an end. They were lovely little people; they were no bigger than children.

60

105

Quotes

If students need more practice with quotes, write a short dialogue on a board or piece of paper so they can see the use of quotation marks as people are speaking. Make sure some of the quotes are two or more sentences long. Also, make some of the quotes "split" quotes - quotes that are interrupted by the speaker's name and said. (The first quote on the student page is a "split" quote.)

Emphasize that there are quotation marks on either side of the quote and that the speaker's name and any "said" words (replied, asked, told, answered, etc.) are NOT inside the quotation marks.

Read the sentences below. If they are quotes, add quotation marks.
"Stay off my lawn," the neighbor said. "I just planted some grass."
Gary replied, "Yes, I will fix the door."
The girl said that she was nine.
"How old are you?" I asked.
My grandpa will tell you that he was a fireman.
Stacy said, "It is almost 5 o'clock. We will have to wait."

Please note that when students are editing, missing quotation marks count as only one error even though they will ALWAYS add them in pairs.

There are 17 errors in this passage.

"What's a Jonah?" asked Harvey, sensing that it was something important.
"A Jonah is anything that bring bad luck. Sometimes it's a man, a boy, or a bucket," said Tom. "There are all kinds of Jonahs, and don't you ever wonder if any of them are true," he told Harvey.
"Well, in my opinion, Harvey is no Jonah," Dan said. "The day after he came aboard, we had the best catch of the day."
The cook threw back his head and interrupted Dan with a strange laugh.
"One day Harvey will be your master, Danny," said the cook.
"Master," he said, pointing to Harvey.
"Man," said the cook, pointing to Dan.
"I'm grateful for the news," said Dan with a laugh. "When?"
"In a few years," answered the cook. "It cannot be avoided." Then he turned to finish peeling potatoes and wouldn't say another word.
Dan said that many things would have to happen before that would take place.

If students need more practice punctuating quotes, write a short dialogue including "split" quotes, commas, and exclamation points/question marks. Let the students punctuate it, and talk through it as they go.

Make sure they understand that a period can NOT be placed between the end of the quote and "____ said." Only a comma, question mark, or exclamation point can be. For example, make sure they never punctuate a sentence like this: **"I want a cracker." Polly said.**

Punctuate the sentences below.
Whitney said that she liked balloons.
I cried, "Wait for me!"
"There aren't," she said, "any more cookies in the jar."
I have a big test tomorrow.
"Can you come over tomorrow?" Sharon asked.
"Wow!" he exclaimed. "That was an awesome circus!"
He looked out the window and said, "That is the biggest bird I've ever seen."

There are 20 errors in this passage.

"Then," spoke Barbicane, "let's take the speed of 2,400 feet each second as our starting point. We'll need to increase it times 15. First, let's talk about the design of the rocket itself."
"What about it?" asked Major Elphiston.
Maston answered, "It must be very large; large enough for whoever lives on the moon to notice."
"Yes," said Barbicane, "and also for another important reason."
"What do you mean?" asked the major.
"I mean, it is not enough to send off a rocket and then forget about it. We must be able to watch it until it reaches the moon."
"What!" yelled the general and the major. "Then you must be planning on making the rocket huge!"
"No," spoke Barbicane, "we'll place a telescope on a high mountain and bring magnification to 48,000. That will bring the moon to within five miles. We will be able to see objects only 9 feet wide."
"Wonderful!" cried J.T. Maston.

Review Time!

There are 20 errors in this passage.

"Yes, Davy," Mr. Micawber said over dinner, "we're leaving. We will move to Plymouth, and we'll start all over."
   "Yes," I thought, "I will start over too. I will run away to my Aunt Betsey's. I know she wished for a boy when I was born... but she is family."

   On the sixth day, I arrived at Aunt Betsey's. At first, she was afraid of my dirty, sunburned face and hands.
   "No boys allowed here!" she cried.
   "Aunt Betsey, it's me... Clara's child. I'm David Copperfield," I said.
   After a long pause, she waved her hand for me to come closer. It was then that I knew I had to make Aunt Betsey like me.

   "I wrote to Mr. Murdstone," Aunt Betsey said one morning. She held up a paper, saying, "Here is his reply, and he's coming for a visit."
   "Oh, no," I said softly.
   "Speak up," Aunt Betsey cried, "smart people don't grumble!"

Homophones

If students need more practice with homophones, try making a list of homophones and writing definitions for them together.

Most of the homophone errors in this book will deal with commonly confused homophones, such as "to - too - two" and "its - it's."

Circle the correct words in the sentences below.

Cindy wanted (to/too/two) ride her new (read/red) bike to the park, but her mother said (know/no).

My brother went to the movies last (knight/night). I went (to/too/two).

(Eye/I) like to (right/write) stories (for/four) my sisters.

Stan was sitting (by/bye) the tree. (Its/It's) leaves were falling all around (him/hymn).

She (new/knew) she was going to like the (new/knew) girl.

If you ever (sea/see) a dragon, the best thing to (do/dew) is simply to walk right up to it and say, "(It's/Its) nice to (meat/meet) you!"

There are 6 errors in this passage.

   Pathfinder saw crouched forms sneaking up (to/too/two) them. He picked Mabel up under his arm and retreated to the shelter. He locked the door quickly and checked to make sure the rooms were empty. There was no one; June had left.
   Outside, the sergeant called that he had been wounded. Pathfinder and Mabel hurried and pulled (hymn/him) inside.
   The sergeant whispered, "Pathfinder, I have (no/know) doubt that you will make Mabel a kind husband. Bless you, my daughter, for doing as I wish." The sergeant laid back, and Mabel bowed her head in prayer.

There are 8 errors in this passage.

   Finally, the door opened. A steward came in carrying a tray of food. Ned could not help himself. He flew into a rage and knocked the man to the floor.

   The men struggled until a voice speaked (spoke) the following words in perfect English: "Calm down, Mr. Land, and thank you, Professor Aronnax, for your help. Now, if you will, please listen to me."

   The man who spoke to the prisoners was the captain of the ship. When he heard the man speak, Ned was startled. He rose suddenly.

   The captain stood with arms folded. He spoke calmly to Ned, Conseil, and the professor. "I owe you three gentlemen an explanation. I was a long time coming to visit you. That was because (I/me) needed to decide what to do with you. You all have caused me much trouble."

   The captain spoke, "It is by an accident which happened on the waters that you (has/have) found my ship. I have the right to treat you as prisoners. I do not owe you your right to freedom."

There are 8 errors in this passage.

Gulliver's ship sailed along for many weeks. The sea was calm, and the weather was warm. Then a great storm came up and the wind blew the ship off course. For days, the ship was tossed by huge waves until, at last, the sailors spotted land.

They needed fresh water, so a small group was sent to the land in a small boat to look for some. Gulliver, wishing to explore, went along.

He walked along the rocky beach for some time, and when he came back, he saw that the sailors were leaving without him, rowing the boat with all (his/their) might toward their ship. Then he saw what had happened to horrify them so. A giant was chasing them!

Gulliver was left behind. He hurried away from the beach. He must find a place to hide! Soon, he found himself in a field of corn. It was huge. Each plant (was/were) as tall as a tree. Suddenly, he saw more giants!

He trembled in fear as they approached. Why had he left the safety of England? Why had he ever left his cozy home? Now he knew how the Lilliputians had felt about him.

69

There are 8 errors in this passage.

Thousands of pounds (was/were) offered in reward for Mr. Hyde. Hyde had disappeared as if he had never lived. Terrible storys were told about him. He had stolen, had often been in fights, and had been cruel to everyone.

A new life began for Dr. Jekyll. He taked (took) great delight in being with his friends. He gave to the poor and was often seen at church. His face seemed to open and brighten, and there was a gleam in his eyes. For more than (to/too/two) months, the doctor was at peace.

Mr. Utterson saw Dr. Jekyll almost every day. Then, one afternoon in January, the door was shut against him. Poole told the lawyer that the doctor was not receiving guests.

70

Prefixes and Suffixes

If students have trouble with prefixes and suffixes, make a list of each. Then have the students help you think of a few words you can make for each prefix and suffix.

Circle any prefixes and suffixes in the sentences below.
She had to return (again) the books to the library.
The boy ran swiftly (adverb) to his tricycle (three).
Dawn thought the previews (before) were funnier (comparative) than the real movie.
My coauthor (together) is very capable (able).
The actress (female) joyfully (full, adverb) read her script.

71

There are 8 errors in this passage.

On October 20, an important contract was signed. It was with the Cold Spring Company. The contract said that this company would be in charge of making the cannon. They would make arrangements to hire all the workers. The work was to be done (buy/by) October 15th of the next year. The cannon would be made in Tampa, Florida.

On September 30, at 3:47 P.M., a message was delivered to Barbicane. It came by cablegram. He opened the envelope and (read/red) the message. His lips turned pale. This is what was written:

            Paris, France

Barbicane   September 30
Tampa, Florida, U.S.A

Replace the cannon shell you have, and put in a lighter shell instead. *I* will go to the moon in it. I will come on the ship named Atlantic.

  Michel Ardan

72

108

There are 6 errors in this passage.

The sun set. The gray of the evening grew into darkness, and Weena was afraid. The Time Traveller, trying to calm her fears, talked until he was (hoarse/horse). He was no longer sure of his direction in the dark, so the Time Traveller decided to rest there until morning. Weena slept, wrapped in his jacket, while he listened for Morlocks.

As soon as dawn came, they started off again. The Time Traveller's foot was so sore that he took off his shoes and throwed (threw) them away. Then he went on, hoping to find something that he could use to break open the base of the white statue. He wanted his Time Machine back and to return to his own time right away.

73

There are 9 errors in this passage.

Meanwhile, Harvey Cheyne, Senior, was in his home in San Diego, California, trying to take care of his business and his wife. Ever since Harvey had been lost at sea, Mrs. Cheyne had become half-mad and needed the care of doctors and nurses. Harvey Cheyne thought of his son often, and his business became less and less important to him.

After three days, fifteen and a half hours, and 2,350 miles, the train arrived at the station. Harvey was waiting for them.

Harvey Cheyne, Senior, looked at his son closely. What he saw pleased him. He remembered what his son had been like - fresh, unhappy, and just plain difficult. The boy in front of him now looked at him with clear, steady eyes. The boy was a pleasant young man who spoke in a voice that said the new Harvey had come to stay.

Harvey's parents visited the wharf the next day. Dan went around introducing the Cheynes to the crew. Mrs. Cheyne was especially happy to meet Manuel when she found out he (had/have) saved her son.

74

There are 9 errors in this passage.

Not only had I lost my job, but my boss wouldn't return Aunt Betsey's money - the money she had paid him for my training. I knew both my aunt and my future wife, Dora, believed that I could become a success. This helped me to rise early the next day to hunt (for/four) a job. Perhaps one of the professors could use the help of someone like (I/me). After all, I once was a schoolboy myself.

I walked to a nearby school and found the head professor's office. "Don't hesitate," I told myself. "Just go in and make your speech."

To my joy, I got the job! I worked days and evenings helping to mark papers. Being at the school made me think of Traddles, and I decided to pay him a visit.

"Hello, old man," Traddles said. "Do you always rise this early in the day?"

I smiled at his sleepy face. "No, but from now on that will be my habit, as I've found a new job."

75

Antonyms and Synonyms

If students need more practice with antonyms, do an oral exercise. You say a word, and then have the student say an antonym. Make sure you pick words with relatively easy antonyms.

For extra practice with synonyms, you can adjust this exercise slightly. You say a word, have the student say a synonym, then you try and come up with another synonym, and so on until someone can't think of another one.

These are also good exercises for students to do with each other, if possible.

Write antonyms and synonyms for the underlined words in the blanks provided. Answers may vary.

	ANTONYMS	SYNONYMS
The boy thought it was hot outside.	cold	warm
The clown was happy.	sad	glad
It was a very big tree.	small	large
The cloud was below the sun.	above	beneath
She ran across the finish line.	walked	sprinted
Karen smiled.	frowned	grinned
The math problem was easy.	hard	simple

109

76

There are 7 errors in this passage.

At the end of <u>C</u>aptain Nemo's guided tour of the *Nautilus*, he pointed to a large map on the wall.

The captain spoke. "We are three hundred miles from <u>J</u>apan. It is twelve noon on November 8<u>,</u> 1867. We will now begin our underwater journey around the world."

Captain Nemo left the professor alone<u>.</u> The professor was deep in thought. He was just about to leave the area when all the lights went out. He heard a noise. There were (to/too/two) sliding panels opening. There was one on each side of the ship.

The professor saw<u>,</u> to his surprise<u>,</u> two large windows. The water outside (was/were) lit up for miles. A beam of light went out as far as the professor<u>'</u>s eyes could see.

"What a view of the ocean floor!" thought the professor. It was like looking out into a giant aquarium.

77

There are 6 errors in this passage.

There was a cry from above. He (Gulliver) heard people moving about. A voice called down, "If (their/there/they're) be anybody below, let them speak!"

"It is <u>I</u>, Lemuel Gulliver! Please save me from this terrible prison<u>!</u>"

"This is the captain! Be of good spirit. You will soon be saved. We must cut a hole in the top of the box," came the answer<u>.</u>

<u>G</u>ulliver protested, "No! One of you must put his finger through the ring! If you lift my box out of the water, I can come through the door!"

Someone laughed. "He must think us giants!"

Soon afterward<u>,</u> a hole was sawed in the top of the box. Gulliver was taken out.

"You are not Brobdingnagians! You are no taller than I!" said Gulliver, amazed.

The captain and ~~sailorss~~ thought him mad.

78

There are 9 errors in this passage.

Mr<u>.</u> Utterson was sitting by his fireside one evening after dinner when he was surprised to receive a visit from Poole.

"Dear me<u>,</u> Poole<u>,</u> what brings you here?" he cried.

Poole looked gloomy. He stood with his shoulders bent and his head hung low.

<u>"</u>What's wrong with you?<u>"</u> asked the lawyer.

"I am very worried about <u>D</u>r. Jekyll," said the butler. "He is shut up again in the laboratory, and I don't like it, sir. I think there's something wrong. Will you come with (I/me) and see for yourself?"

Mr. Utterson's only answer was to rise and get his hat and coat. A look of relief appeared on Poole<u>'</u>s face.

It was a cold<u>,</u> gloomy night in <u>M</u>arch. Dark clouds raced across the moon as the wind began to rage. Mr. Utterson shivered. Wondered what horror he might find at Dr. Jekyll's.

79

There are 6 errors in this passage.

The cannon that would shoot three ~~mans~~ to the moon had been finished. Michel Ardan<u>,</u> the artist and astronaut, wanted some changes made to the space capsule's design. He wanted to (has/have) more room overhead. He felt cramped inside. He felt like a squirrel in a cage<u>.</u> He got in touch with the company who builded (built) the capsule and asked them to make a few changes. They said (they/them) would check the design and make the changes.

Ardan<u>,</u> Barbicane<u>,</u> and Captain Nicholl were the three astronauts. They waited for all to be ready. The huge silver capsule sparkled in the sunlight.

80

110

Expressive Words

This is another subject where you can do some oral exercises, simply by saying a "dull" adjective, verb, or noun and having the students answer back with a more expressive word.

Rewrite the sentences replacing nouns, verbs, and adjectives with more exciting, expressive words. Answers will vary.

The girl laughed at the funny monkeys.
The teenage girl chuckled at the amusing monkeys.
Casey said, "The grass is getting very long."
Casey reported, "The grass is getting extremely long."
My brother says that sports are fun.
My older brother insists that sports are enjoyable.
The little hamster ate his food.
The tiny hamster gobbled up his seeds.
I picked red flowers to give to my friend.
I picked ruby red roses to present to my best friend.
The rain fell against my window.
The sleet slammed against my bedroom window.
Derek ran to the old mailbox.
Derek raced to the ancient mailbox.
The blue car drove by our small house.
The royal blue car whizzed by our modest house.

81

There are 7 errors in this passage.

Pathfinder decided Jasper must talk to Mabel after her father was buried. Mabel was left in Pathfinder's care. It was (his/their) duty to see the girl choose her own happiness.

On the day they were to leave the island, Pathfinder took Mabel and Jasper to a fallen log and told them to sit down. He began by saying that Mabel agreed to be his wife without knowing Jasper's feelings.

"Pathfinder!" Mabel gasped and turned deathly pale.

"I've been talking with Jasper. It seems we both (think/thinks) alike when it comes to you."

Tear after tear runned (ran) down the girl's cheeks. "I've promised my father..." She bowed her head.

Mabel's shoulders shook with silent cries. Finally, she looked at Jasper to see if all Pathfinder said was true. She saw that it was.

It was time to go. Pathfinder took Mabel's hands, his eyes wet with tears. "Jasper, be happy and take good care of her."

Pathfinder waved good-bye.

82

There are 9 errors in this passage.

Back through time he flew, until at last he was in (him/his) own laboratory on the same day he had left it. He heard people talking in the next room and knew that we, his dinner guests, must be there. His feet still sore, he limped in to join us.

This was the story that our friend, the Time Traveller, told us as we sat at his dinner table that night. As he'd warned us, it was hard to believe, but how else could we explain his cuts, scratches, and bloody socks?

The next morning I went alone to the Time Traveller's house.

For one second I thought I saw the Time Traveller on his machine, but both disappeared like ghosts before my eyes. The laboratory was empty. Eager to see what new story my friend would bring back, I waited as long as I could. He didn't come back. Three years (has/have) passed, and he still hasn't returned.

83

There are 8 errors in this passage.

Several years later, on the West Coast, Dan and Harvey met again. Dan was standing in front of the Cheyne's house in California when Harvey rode in on his horse.

"Hello, Dan!"

"Hello, Harve!"

"What's the best with you?" asked Harvey.

Dan told Harvey that he (was/were) going to be the second mate on the next trip of a freighter owned by the Cheynes. Harvey told Dan that he was coming into the business for good in the fall and would be taking over the freighters.

The ex-cook from the *We're Here* comed (came) out to take Harvey's horse.

"Man," he said, pointing to Dan. "Master," he said, as he pointed to Harvey. "Do you remember what I said on the *We're Here*, Dan Troop?" asked the cook.

"It does look like that's the way things are (right/write) now," said Dan.

84

111

There are 8 errors in this passage.

I was gone for months, and before I knew it, a year had passed. Agnes wrote me many letters filled with news about Aunt Betsey, Traddles, and Micawber. Aunt Betsey was fine, and Agnes had helped her plant a garden. Traddles now had his own law business. I had to laugh when I (red/read) that Micawber now worked for Traddles. What a pair these two made! I hoped Traddles would keep Micawber out of trouble.

My writing was going very well, and more and more people knew my name. My storys were being read all over the world now. I thought about how pleased Mama and Dora and even Steerforth would be with me. They were gone, as were so many others - Ham, the baby, and Dora's father. I thought of the Peggottys who had moved so far away. I thought of the many troubles I went through while growing up. Now that some time has passed, I (feel/feels) I have changed in some way.

Sentence Combining

If students need more practice with sentence combining, ask them questions like this: "What information in this sentence is new information that needs to be included, and what information is repeated and unneccessary?" "How can we fit the new information into the old sentence?" Once they can identify the new information in each sentence, they can combine those parts to form one complete sentence. If necessary, write some additional series of short sentences until they are able to combine them without any problems.

Combine each group of sentences below into one sentence.
I like baseball. I like football. I also like volleyball.
I like baseball, football, and volleyball.
She picked out a new watch. It was a black watch. The wristband was made of leather.
She picked out a new black watch with a leather wristband.
The boy went to the pet store. The boy was twelve years old. He went to the pet store to watch the fish.
The twelve-year old boy went to the pet store to watch the fish.
For supper we are having spaghetti. There is also garlic bread.
For supper we are having spaghetti and garlic bread.
The airplane had many seats. The seats were blue. The seats were also striped.
The airplane had many blue striped seats.

There are 9 errors in this passage.

As Mr. Utterson read Dr. Lanyon's letter, his heart was beating so fast that he thought it would explode.

(The following is the letter from Dr. Lanyon.)

Midnight had just rung over London when there came a soft knock on my door. I heard the sound of a freight horn. A short man was standing in the shadows.

"Did Dr. Jekyll send you?" I asked. He told me yes, and I bid him enter. When he stepped into the light, I must say, I was struck by the wild look on his face.

He took the drugs from Dr. Jekyll's strange cargo and put them in the glass.

He put the glass to his lips and drank. He cried out, staggered, and grabbed at the table.

"Oh, no!" I screamed again and again, for before my eyes, there stood Henry Jekyll!

I will say but one last thing, Utterson, and try to believe it. The creature who came to my house that night and turned into Henry Jekyll was none other than Mr. Hyde.

There are 8 errors in this passage.

A few months after returning to England, Lemuel Gulliver sailed away again. What other wonders would he find across the seas?

"What is this place?" asked Gulliver.
"Laputa," came the answer.
Gulliver looked around. What a strange place! What strange people! Their heads were bent to the right or left. Their clothes were covered with suns, moons, and stars. They spent all (his/their) time thinking and studying. It seemed they (was/were) only interested in arithmetic and music. Yet all their learning seemed to cause them trouble.

Gulliver left Laputa the same way he came, by climbing down a long chain. He found himself in a new country called Balnibarbi.
The Balnibarbians had no common sense. They didn't know a good idea from a bad one. This Gulliver learned when he visited the city of Lagado, where a center of learning was opened.
Gulliver was amazed by what he saw (their/there/they're). People were working hard and getting nowhere! Great amounts of money were being spent on all kinds of foolish ideas.

There are 7 errors in this passage.

The three astronauts arrived. Addressing the crowd, Michel Ardan said, "We are ready to make our way into space!"
The crowd roared again as they waved to the crew.
"Thank you all (for/four) coming," added Barbicane. He was pleased at the number of ~~persons~~ who supported (there/their/they're) efforts.
Captain Nicholl, the third astronaut, was unusually quiet. He looked at the crowd with tears of joy in his eyes. He, like Barbicane, was pleased that so many had come to see them off. He was upset that he might never see any of them again.

"You are heroes!" the crowd shouted. (They/Them) yelled so loud that the music being played could hardly be heard. The excitement seemed to grow with every passing moment.

The three astronauts stepped into a big, wire cage. Then the door closed.

A loud noise came from below that was louder than any sound ever heard before. The ground shaked (shook) like an earthquake as smoke and fire shot out of the ground. Only a few people saw the capsule shoot into the air. It (has/had) happened so fast!

89

Final Examination

There are 12 errors in this passage.

Ned rushed into the professor's cabin one day and shouted to him, "We are heading south to Antarctica and the South Pole."
At the South Pole, they came upon another adventure with icy waters and whales. There, Captain Nemo put up a black flag with an "N" on it. Spoke loudly for all to hear.
"Today, March 21, 1868, I, Captain Nemo, have reached the South Pole. I now claim it as mine."
After a few more adventures, the professor and Ned were no longer comfortable being on the *Nautilus*. They realized (them/they) could no longer stay on the ship. They wanted to go home.

Ned and the professor planned their escape right away. They headed for the small boat. They lowered the boat down into the water. Freedom was near.
Something happened. The *Nautilus* and the small boat carrying Ned, the professor, and Conseil were caught up in the middle of a whirlpool.
The professor blacked out. The next thing he knew, he, Ned, and Conseil were in a fisherman's cabin off the coast of Norway. He did not know what happened. A miracle maybe - or an act of God? The professor had (no/know) answers.

90